Palestine in a World on Fire

PALESTINE
in a World on Fire

Edited by Katherine Natanel and Ilan Pappé

Haymarket Books
Chicago, IL

Published in 2024 by
Haymarket Books
P.O. Box 180165
Chicago, IL 60618
www.haymarketbooks.org

ISBN: 9798888902585

Distributed to the trade in the US through Consortium Book Sales
and Distribution (www.cbsd.com) and internationally through In-
gram Publisher Services International (www.ingramcontent.com).

This book was published with the generous support of Lannan Foundation, Wallace Action Fund, and Marguerite Casey Foundation.

Special discounts are available for bulk purchases by organizations
and institutions. Please email info@haymarketbooks.org for more
information.

Cover artwork © Rand Hammoud. Cover design by Jamie Kerry.

Printed in Canada by union labor.

Library of Congress Cataloging-in-Publication data is available.

10 9 8 7 6 5 4 3 2 1

CONTENTS

INTRODUCTION

We are living in a world on fire. Ignited by wars and global warming, fires burn forests, fields, and homes. Fueled by hate and racist ideologies, fires feed on despair, authoritarianism, colonialism, crime, oppression, and poverty. In 2019, fire swept across the globe in the form of a pandemic, bringing death and misery to staggering numbers of people who live in regions where public health has been decimated by neoliberal policies and replaced by unaffordable (private) services.

Millions of people are destitute because of these infernos, living with constant fear and in many cases forced to seek life elsewhere. The outcome is the largest movement of refugees the world has witnessed since the Second World War. Depictions of scorched gray, white, and black landscapes in films of a postnuclear or postpandemic world are not incidental; real and metaphorical fires threaten our world. However, they are not evenly spread. The Global South is seared by flames of destruction more deeply and regularly than the Global North, which exists as if shielded from future disasters by borders, immigration policies, and physical barriers. Lives are lived, suspended, and lost in the im/balance.

Yet people are not solely victims of the world ablaze. Rather, they show incredible agency and resilience in the face of catastrophe. In this century, those who refuse to continue living under conditions of colonialism, racism, and inequality communicate and coordinate— they meet one another, whether physically or virtually, to build solidarity movements. Raising political awareness, analyzing injustice, exposing the roles of capitalism and imperialism, questioning the relationship between knowledge and power structures—shared concerns about *how we live* and *who we are* become tools for fighting the fires in front of us.

Palestine in a World on Fire brings together leading voices in the struggle to name, confront, and redress the global crises with/in which we live. These conversations invite us to reflect on how the climate emergency, planetary racism, and public health intersect with neoliberalism, migration, and border policies. We are encouraged to think deeply about indigeneity, subalternity, and Third World feminisms in relation to colonialism, imperialism, and right-wing nationalisms. We are compelled to question the meaning of academic freedom in the context of the Prevent duty, the International Holocaust Remembrance Alliance definition of antisemitism, and the ongoing Nakba in Palestine.

As we revise our introduction in May 2024, Palestine is on fire. Cities, neighborhoods, camps, homes, and loved ones in Gaza are being lost to aerial bombardment, ground assault, strategic deprivation, and forced migration in almost incomprehensible numbers. Journalists, activists, educators, and organizers are being detained and silenced within the borders of the Israeli state for daring to challenge the narratives that justify genocide. Young people in the West Bank are being killed by sniper fire from Israeli soldiers, or under the wheels of Palestinian Authority armored vehicles, for protesting the collusion between these two forces. While our conversation series sought to center Palestine as a crucial entry point for understanding and confronting the global crises named above, today we feel even more certainty in arguing that *Palestine is the point*. Palestine, Palestinians, and their supporters "can teach us to live and struggle in the current conjecture,"[1] but only to the extent that we rise to our responsibility to fight alongside them, to insist on talking, seeing, and doing when those in positions of power would have it otherwise. Perhaps never has it felt so urgent, as we witness ethnic cleansing unfolding before our eyes.

Within the pages that follow, we trace the story of our conversation series and explore what these dialogues might teach us about decolonization as a material, intellectual, and creative practice. Our introduction gleans "tools" from honest and critical encounters, with the understanding that true decolonization will respond to the context from which it erupts—there is no single path to liberation, and it is not our place to suggest this. Instead, we distill lessons through which strategies and tactics might be developed based on the knowledge shared by scholars, organizers, activists, and educators whose commitment to Palestine shines as a guiding light. It is with awe and humility that we recognize how a young generation is already taking up these lessons and tools, actualizing and sharpening them in the service of resistance and solidarity. Ignited by the community at Columbia University and spreading rapidly to campuses around the world, the fire of the student encampments burns brightly, providing inspiration and hope in this moment of darkness. These activists ensure that Palestine will not be denied or forgotten, and that support for its people will only grow.

HOW IT BEGAN

From January 2021 through September 2022, we reached out to public intellectuals from across the globe and conducted eleven online conversations, making use of the digital platforms that became "everyday" during the height of the COVID-19 pandemic. Hosted by the Institute of Arab and Islamic Studies, University of Exeter, these events were attended by two hundred to seven hundred online viewers on a given night and later made available as recordings on YouTube for access by organizers, activists, scholars, and educators. They take shape here as an edited written volume, in hopes of cultivating and sharing knowledge in another form.

As often happens, the emergence of the Palestine conversation series is a story of how discrete processes, seemingly disconnected, fused together. One process was the rapid spread of the COVID-19 pandemic, which brought online discussion platforms to the fore; these technologies connected us across time and space, even while "locked down" in our homes. The pandemic also unexpectedly made people much more available—speakers who would ordinarily need to be booked months, if not years, in advance to join events in person were suddenly able to jump on calls to share their wisdom and experience. We owe credit to how people innovated and maneuvered in conditions of uncertainty and loss, finding ways to connect and generously share their time.

A second development was the emergence of a new network at the University of Exeter: the Exeter Decolonizing Network (EDN). EDN was formed in 2019 as a collective of staff and students whose intellectual, creative, and political work focuses on decoloniality and antiracism. Members of EDN understand and engage in decolonization as an intersectional politics, confronting colonialism and racism as these modes of violence articulate with capitalism, heteropatriarchy, transphobia, ableism, Islamophobia, and more. EDN is both a response and action group—holding the university accountable to its stated values and commitments while coordinating events and activities that support decolonial approaches to teaching, learning, research, and organizing. Recognizing the importance of Palestine to local and global struggles for decolonization, EDN mobilized its expansive network to facilitate and support the conversation series.

The final development was a renewed interest among British universities in Black history, which surged in the wake of George Floyd's murder in Minneapolis, Minnesota (USA), in May 2020 and the toppling of Edward Colston's statue in Bristol (UK) in June of the same year.[2] These events drew attention to Black Lives Matter (BLM) as a movement for justice and liberation, animated by activists organizing on local and global stages. BLM demands accountability for police and historical violence as aspects of a broad systemic matrix, directing attention to how racism is cultural and structural. In doing so, BLM implicates spaces of teaching and learning—including universities—as sites of racialized violence and radical change. The University of Exeter responded to pressure from students, staff, and the local community by funding and promoting activities that advance the work of antiracism and decolonization on campus and beyond.

Through this confluence of actors and events, we opened our conversation series in January 2021 with Angela Y. Davis.[3] While the interview transcript included in this volume relays her exchange with Ilan, it cannot capture the excitement in our (virtual) room with a sold-out Zoom audience and over four hundred additional attendees on YouTube.[4] In that evening and the dialogues that followed, we were graced with the courage, wisdom, and imagination of intellectual and political leaders. We learned from scholars, educators, and organizers who toil tirelessly and actively participate in struggles for justice, liberation, and self-determination—in their local communities, in Palestine, and across the globe.

Our guests have devoted their careers and lifelong activism to unearthing the structures and discourses that maintain political violence, white supremacy, heteropatriarchy, and neoliberal capitalism. They shared knowledge gained from rigorous research, difficult discussions, self-reflection, and investment in initiatives that refuse the status quo. Each speaker also shares a belief in the transformative potential of dialogue. Their conversations with Ilan demonstrate how the exchange of ideas and experiences does not solely enrich our understanding of the past and present—rather, discussion enables us to imagine new futures.

The bleakness of our present time is clear. Yet so is the urgency with which we must confront it. The conversations that compose *Palestine in a World on Fire* grapple with financial crises and regional uprisings, national identity and sectarianism, vaccination policies and social welfare, fascism and the rise of the extreme right, the future of the left and coalitional politics, immigration policy and border violence, how conflict and death are represented in global media, and the limits of personal empathy and political mobilization. However, every exchange ended on a note of hope—as a political emotion, a foundation of community, and a catalyst of action. In these moments, an energy was felt across time and space among organizers, speakers, and attendees; distances dissolved, and we stepped forward, together.

PALESTINE IN THE WORLD

For more than two years, we were graced with the time and attention of scholar-activists whose work is at once intellectually incisive and politically useful. Following their inspiration, this section considers what we might take away from the conversation series as a whole—the lessons that we might carry with us in the struggle for decolonization.[5] Here we reflect on their offerings as imperatives that we must contemplate and actualize as we commit to liberation, self-determination, and justice as material practices. While the first "lesson" below draws extensively on Ilan's experience in cultivating historiographical knowledge of Palestine, the subsequent sections are driven by the voices of our guests. Their words constitute the core of the series' thematic teachings, with limited mediation from us as editors. In doing so, we underline the importance of memory, experience, dialogue, inquiry, and imagination as forms of knowledge—and we insist on the presence and significance of Palestine in the world.

First Lesson: Learn Your History

From Edward Said's "Permission to Narrate" to Rana Barakat's "Writing/Righting Palestine Studies," much scholarly attention and activist energy has been devoted to the question of *who tells the story* of Palestine.[6] For the speakers in our series, this is not solely a matter of discourse or intellectual pursuit; the struggle to articulate Palestine's past, present, and future is both existential and material.

Ilan spoke with each of our guests about the role of narrative, in connection to Palestine and the broader movement for decolonization. Sustained by academic work, narratives influence school curricula, mainstream media discourses and reportage, cultural productions, and political policy. As seen in Palestine, Israel invests an incredible amount of energy and resources in attempting to validate its territorial claims and justify its policies, often on the basis of "scientific" academic research. In many ways, the contest over narrative can be seen as a zero-sum game, where acceptance or successful validation undermines—and even prevents—any counterclaims. Gabor Maté reminded us of the depth and pervasiveness of this phenomenon:

> If you ask the average Israeli, Canadian, or British person, "Put together three intelligent sentences about the history of Palestine," they couldn't do it. You can ask the average British person, whose country participated in the invasion of Iraq with the death of over half a million people, "Put

together three intelligent sentences on the history of Iraq or of Afghanistan." Or right now, "Give me three intelligent sentences about the history of Ukraine in the last ten years." They couldn't do it. Because an ingrained passivity is built into the social character, which serves the interest of the social-political structure that it is designed to perpetuate.

While Israel has long held the upper hand when it comes to representation in global mainstream media, political decision-making, and (Western) public opinion, the presence and mounting strength of the Palestinian story galvanizes support for liberation. Through the conversation series, we sought to provide a stage upon which this story—or rather these multiple Palestinian stories—could be shared and linked to nodes in other anticolonial narratives and decolonial struggles. In this way, the history of a place and people is never isolated; we are always already connected.

In the case of Palestine, a robust field of scholarly knowledge enables us to access and engage—to learn—that history in part through a process of institutionalization. Palestine studies, as a discipline, makes knowable the stakes in the contest over narrative; the richness of Palestinian political, intellectual, and social life; how settler-colonial violence is experienced and resisted; and what a decolonial future might look like. Told one way, this disciplinary story is tied to the emergence of other fields of study: Israel studies and Jewish studies. It is indeed possible to see Palestine studies taking shape as a decolonial antidote to a project of erasure and denial. These roots tell the story of a riposte, an insistence on presence and audibility—a knowledge project as a strategy for survival. Yet narrating the emergence of Palestine studies as enabled by the development of Israel studies risks reproducing the violence that Palestinian scholars, activists, educators, and organizers are fighting to make known. Tying Palestine studies so firmly to Israel studies enacts a form of epistemic violence that we are obligated to acknowledge and confront if we are truly committed to working in decolonial and anticolonial ways.

As we learned from those who gave life to our series, "histories shape what surfaces"—whether objects, sensations, or political realities.[7] Learning our history means detailing a trajectory of Palestine studies that honors the wisdom, courage, and vision of those who give substance and meaning to an academic discipline as practice of liberation and self-determination. The Nakba constitutes a watershed moment that rattled every aspect of Palestinian life, including the scholarly and academic structures that emerged during the British mandate. Rather than ending with the establishment of the Israeli state, the Nakba is ongoing—al-Nakba al-mustamirrah[8]—meaning that the cultivation and sharing of knowledge remains a target for elimination, whether through destruction, omission, or assimilation. And yet a rich intellectual practice has persisted, growing in depth and driven in part by noninstitutionalized ways of knowing. Palestine studies owes credit to storytelling, embodied memory, and artistic expression as much as academic labor.[9]

In the years after 1948, energy and resources were dedicated to (re)building scholarly institutions in sites that circumvented territorial control and in ways that defied the project of erasure. Two major Palestinian research bodies appeared in Beirut, Lebanon, in the space of two years: the Institute of Palestine Studies (1963) and the PLO's Palestine Research Center (1965). Between 1965 and 1982, forty researchers associated with the Palestine Research Center produced more than three hundred publications, creating the foundational body of work for a discipline.[10] Knowledge of and in the Arabic-speaking world was brought to English-language audiences by the Institute for Palestine Studies' publication of the *Journal of Palestine Studies* in 1971, as well as its establishment of a branch in Washington, DC, in 1983. This investment in research and publication emerged in the context of sustained attacks on dispersed Palestinian archives and the continuing oppression of academic life in the occupied territories. In places like Beirut and Jerusalem, repositories of collective knowledge faced looting, seizure, and destruction—often at the hands of the Israeli state. Yet these concerted attempts at further dispossession and erasure have failed to deter generation after generation of Palestinian scholars from reconstructing the past, analyzing the present, and imagining the future, wherever they may be.

The effort to cultivate, protect, and circulate knowledge of Palestine has been enriched by the development of intersectional fields of inquiry elsewhere, including cultural, decolonial, feminist, Indigenous, Marxist, and postcolonial studies. On these broad shoulders rests the present field of Palestine studies, now a recognized area of inquiry in a growing number of academic centers around the world. Between 2010 and 2020, centers, units, and projects of Palestine studies were opened at Brown and Columbia universities in the United States; University of Cambridge, Oxford University, SOAS, and the University of Exeter in the United Kingdom; and most recently at the University of Waterloo in Canada. Similar initiatives have appeared in Qatar, Malaysia, Mexico, Colombia, and Argentina, complementing a growing interest in the Arab world and the development of dedicated academic programs. By working across contexts and struggles, researchers, educators, and organizers are speaking to new forms of solidarity, means of resistance, and imaginations of the future.

And yet we are still listening to and learning from Khalil, the protagonist of Elias Khoury's *Bab al-Shams* (*Gate of the Sun*), who underlines the stakes of this effort:

I'm scared of a history that has only one version. History has dozens of versions, and for it to ossify into only one leads only to death. We mustn't see ourselves only in their mirror, for they're prisoners of one story, as though that story had abbreviated and ossified them . . . You mustn't become just one story . . . I see you as a man who betrays and repents and loves and fears and dies. This is the only way if we're not to ossify and die.

Second Lesson: Develop an Old/New Language

Learning our history and shifting the story requires a specific vocabulary, a way of reaching and moving people. When we asked our first guest, Angela Y. Davis, what the nature of this vocabulary might be, we were blessed with a clear and powerful reply:

We need a new lexicon, we need new vocabularies. And that can be transformative. I'm simply thinking about the fact that when many of us first began to do abolitionist work around prisons, we asked ourselves how we could begin to encourage a critical stance toward the assumption that crime is responsible for the massive prison build-up. How can we disarticulate crime and punishment, and bring a popular understanding of the role that racism and capitalism play in mass incarceration? And we began to use the term "prison industrial complex." That helped to shift the conversation away from individuals who committed crimes and therefore deserved punishment, to the ways in which economic and political systems were very much responsible for this growth in the numbers of people incarcerated.[11]

Through her experience of abolitionist work in the United States, Davis makes knowable how shifts in language or terminology can radically transform public knowledge—shaping not only how people speak, but also where they see power and the structures it creates. She points to a precedent that those working toward abolition and decolonization in other contexts can take up, a story to learn from and share as they confront macro-political power and ingrained social passivity.

As the Palestine conversation series unfolded, our speakers added layers to this lexicon of transformation. Many invoked an academic language built through efforts in gender, Indigenous, and subaltern studies to question the hegemonic frameworks and phrases that dominate public discussion and scholarly research. Drawing on their changing relationship to feminism, Judith Butler cautioned against the impulse to universalize terminology or assume shared concerns in movements and struggles:

> There's no single model that we can develop in one part of the world and impose upon the other ... I have emerged in the last thirty years through US feminism, which too often thought that feminist theory takes place in English. That whatever is said in English is therefore universally true! This elaborates a kind of cultural imperialism at the level of language, but even the term "gender" is not easily translatable. Many feminists have had to push back on the term gender, or to find innovations within their own languages because it doesn't fit with the syntax or perhaps it's not the central category for feminist concerns.

From this history of feminist scholarly critique and organizing, we learn about the limits of language and its entanglement with power. At the same time, we are reminded of the potential for words to *do work* in the service of justice. Women "push back" and "find innovations" through drawing on their own languages and bringing this richness of experience to the struggle. Butler also underlined the importance of engaging with what exists as we develop a lexicon, signaling how the new is often old or familiar:

> For me, the work of linguistic and cultural translation is key. We're constantly learning! Feminism has not just been about the equality of women, or the emancipation of women from violence and subordination. It has also been a question: What is it to be a woman, or how is that category built, regulated, or reproduced? And that means that the category is being rearticulated through time.

This rearticulation of categories and language is not solely the domain of scholars, however. Everyday life, familiar interactions, and mundane occurrences can also provide us with a vocabulary of transformation. Nadera Shalhoub-Kevorkian drew on the voices and words of children, those indomitable askers of questions, insisting that we attend to their language as we seek to build our own:

> Following the assassination of Shireen Abu Akleh, I went to Haret al-Sa'diyya and there was a little girl, seven or eight years old, and a large group of soldiers. The soldiers were talking and suddenly she started calling her friend in a loud voice, "Fattoum! Fattoum! Come play hide-and-seek!" And she looked at the soldiers, telling them in a loud voice, "If you killed Shireen Abu Akleh, do you think I'm not going to play hide-and-seek? . . . If you fill the grave-yards with our bones, do you think we're not going to play hide-and-seek?" And she kept on calling Fattoum.

Listen, just hearing her voice. This is a voice of clear defiance, of resistance, of refusal of power. I look at those things that maybe many people would pass and wouldn't notice—her voice and her call for Fattoum. . . . We are trying to understand but also respect children's walk to school, children's language—how they speak *life* when the system speaks death and unchilding.

Grounded in academic labor and everyday life, expressed in analytical and defiant tones, our language can name past and present injustices—and enable us to develop imaginative tools for rebuilding the world.

Third Lesson: Question How Things Work

Our commitment to learning history and building an old/new vocabulary must be driven by a particular kind of intellectual and political curiosity—one that compels us to dig beneath the surface of appearances. Each conversation pushed past a "simple" answer to pursue knowledge of the complex logics, mechanisms, and ideologies that sustain political violence and inequality. In doing so, our guests drew attention to how connections across contexts and scales underpin the status quo, unearthing often deeply woven coordination and complicities.

Every transcript in our edited volume does this precise work of excavation at length, elucidating *how things work*, from the global economy to legal frameworks and governmental responses to the COVID-19 pandemic. As we follow these stories, we learn about the entanglements and agreements that fuel the world's fires—even while political leaders claim to be fighting them. Yanis Varoufakis spoke to the interconnection among crises by grounding his reflections in an approach to economics that invites questioning. This was not the narrow, individualist view that characterizes neoliberalism, but a way of understanding the content, flow, accumulation, and effects of capital that attends to the collective:

> We need to start talking about the historical necessity of shedding light on events that seemed indecipherable. . . . What is it that gives rise to wealth creation? How is income distributed? What is the mechanism by which competition leads to innovation, innovation leads to capital accumulation, capital accumulation leads to investment, investment leads to technical progress, technical progress leads to social ruptures, and so on? These were the big questions that the first economists tackled, without actually calling themselves economists.

Varoufakis is concerned with the *ideas* of economics—its global history—as central to its contemporary practice. By questioning how the current frame became dominant, we become aware of a discrepancy between economics as a "holistic organic approach" and the mathematized, scientific, professionalized field it is today. The devastating effect of this "disengagement between economic theory and really existing capitalism" was felt globally in 2008, when economic models proved incapable of forecasting crisis. Varoufakis's ideas clearly resonate in Palestine when we ask how flows of capital and power sustain Israeli settler colonialism; but his warning about disengagement is just as instructive:

> You wrote, "It seems that even the most horrendous crimes, such as the genocide in Gaza, are treated as disparate events; unconnected to anything that happened in the past, and not associated with any ideology or system." That is racism

in action. The moment you take just the figures of a conflict out of the context of ongoing ethnic cleansing, of pushing a native people off their land. The moment you're allowed to get away without commenting on this underlying project is when you become complicit with the crime being perpetrated.

Nadine El-Enany followed this thread further, challenging us to question what is taken for granted with a focus on how the rule of law is implicated in violence. By adopting the language of "mythology," El-Enany traced connections between Britain and Israel while revealing cracks in their political claims:

> In my work I tried to dispel the myth that Britain is a post-imperial, legitimately bordered, sovereign nation-state. Challenging this myth is the first step toward a project of practically dismantling the violent border regime. The myth that Israel is a democratic state has a similar kind of cataclysmic power in how we begin to understand, or not understand, particular situations. . . . It is important to dwell on the status and power of these kinds of myths because they are actually what obstruct the very kind of solidarity that Palestinians are calling for, and that we are calling for—the kind that supports the Palestinian struggle for liberation.

This is a profoundly different story about the power and legitimacy of states than the narratives promoted through mainstream media and political discourse. In turning a sharp curiosity toward what is accepted as truth, El-Enany names the constructions, norms, and relations that underpin our present political realities. While we gain new understanding of how logics and mechanisms animate and maintain power, we also become aware of their contradictions:

This is how myths work, because Israel cannot be a democratic state and be an apartheid state—it cannot be a democratic state and a settler-colonial power at the same time. Britain cannot be a domestic space of colonialism and also a postimperial, legitimately bordered, sovereign nation-state. Because there are certain principles that underlie a democratic state, like the rule of law and equality before the law.

These principles cannot be sustained in a context in which a section of the population is oppressed, regarded and treated as nonhuman, subject to targeted state violence and murder daily. Where state laws and policies are specifically designed to promote and propagate the supremacy of one section of the population. These laws and policies are also designed to cleanse the land of another section of the population through police and military violence, evictions, the destruction and occupation of property, allowing violent groups to torment people and act with impunity, controlling the economy to ensure a specific part cannot survive, thrive, or flourish. And through legal judgments, which replicate and legitimize that violence.

Through questioning foundational claims, El-Enany makes visible the threads connecting state power, violence, political policy, and legal judgments in Britain and Palestine. However, this is not solely the work of diagnosis; rather, we begin to see a clear basis for the kind of solidarity that supports struggles for justice and liberation. Asking and understanding *how things work*—identifying logics, mechanisms, connections, discrepancies, and contradictions—means that we might better challenge the knowledge and structures that produce and sustain violence. We are given targets for action.

Fourth Lesson: Feel Your Way

What brought El-Enany to the framing of mythology and Varoufakis to an awareness of disengagement? What compelled them to
ask *how things work* to maintain power and how the world might
be otherwise? Intellectual curiosity and political determination,
certainly. However, the guests in our series point to other energies
that motivate the search for knowledge and movements for transformation: sensation and emotion.

It is not a far stretch to suggest that intuition attuned El-Enany
to the power of myths in political claim-making, or that discomfort
drove Varoufakis to ask whether the history of economic thought
inevitably leads to crisis and complicity. Emerging as suspicion,
worry, or frustration, the feeling that *things are not right* animates
intellectual inquiry as it serves the project of material decolonization. While institutional gatekeepers have largely managed to
exclude emotion and sensation from the realm of "knowledge,"
these ways of being and making meaning have long been sources
of individual and collective wisdom.[12]

Emotion and sensation shaped the conversation series in powerful ways, not least as our topics and speakers responded to ongoing violence in Palestine and around the world. Guests reached
back for memories, shared their lived experiences, and dared to
imagine—this wisdom was conveyed with warmth, honesty,
anger, sadness, and hope. With pride we write that the events were
marked by fearlessness and friendship. While feeling enriched the
atmosphere of exchange, it also sharpened and deepened our analysis of settler-colonial violence. For the final conversation, Nadera
Shalhoub-Kevorkian joined us from her home in the Old City of
Jerusalem, "where daily military occupation, ethnic cleansing,
apartheid, dispossession, and kill-ability is confronted with Palestinians' livability, togetherness, joy, love, and growing solidarity

here and around the world." Her words forced us to face the reality of how Palestinian women's bodies are "used and abused" by the settler-colonial project—whether alive or dead. Harrowing narratives relayed experiences of Israeli control that target not only land and community but also psyche and senses:

> By occupation of the senses, I refer to the technologies that are managing the language, the sight, the sound, the time, the light. Come here and listen to the darkness, look at the light and the space in the colony! It is the administration of who acts, who speaks, who gives birth and how. Who walks, who moves, who drives where and how. What kind of language, music, smells, marches, colors, cultures, and scenes are promoted or inscribed over spaces. . . .
>
> My inquiry is concerned with the ways in which the settler colony uses sensory stimuli in a confrontational manner with the aim of invading the experience of the colonized, producing exclusivity and hegemony on the basis of one culture, one religion, one national and security claim.

Paying attention to sensation and emotion—feeling our way—enables us to name and know violence better, understanding how it permeates both life and death. But also it reminds us of Fattoum and her friend, whose call to play hide-and-seek rings out as a refusal of power.

Taking feeling seriously can result in clarity of vision and precision of analysis, as demonstrated by Shalhoub-Kevorkian; this is indispensable for projects of decolonization. However, making space for emotion and sensation can also reveal ambiguities and tensions that complicate this work.[13] Judith Butler alerted us to the pitfalls of affinity in their reflection on the struggle to overcome dehumanization:

I sometimes worry about compassion, that it involves setting up identification: "These other people are just like me." Just as I suffer, so others suffer. Just as my people suffer, so others suffer. That is a principle of equality and it's an important one, but there's also a different history. If I really want to be affected by the catastrophe of the ongoing Nakba, if I want to make myself open to the suffering of others, it may be that I should not assume an absolute parallelism between the lives of others and my life. . . . As you say, rightly, "How do we convince people, persuade people, or get them to understand this quite systematic dehumanization of Palestinians?" That's a perfectly great question. The problem I see is that there's an idea of the human that's lodged within the critique of dehumanization. If Palestinians or non-Palestinians want to say, "Palestinians are human just like everyone else," which version of the human are we invoking at that moment?

Through their discomfort—with compassion, identification, and notions of "the human"—Butler urges us to (re-)consider the grounds on which solidarities are built. Pity, charity, and compassion prove unstable and insincere. Instead, the struggle calls for "[recognizing] Palestinians as empowered, purposive peoples with desires and goals of their own, and as being completely invested and engaged in the project of their own liberation in that context."

Feeling our way in the practice of material decolonization means holding these things together: the pain of occupation in its fullest sense and the necessary discomfort of solidarity work. The result must not be paralysis, but a renewed commitment to grapple with these tensions—as crucial to liberation.

Fifth Lesson: Acknowledge Failure

Staying with pain and discomfort in our political, intellectual, and creative work requires more than a view that looks beyond our own feelings or interests to train focus on the collective horizon. Somewhat surprisingly, we learned from our guests about the importance of acknowledging failure. These prominent figures in the worlds of scholarship, activism, education, and organizing were honest about how frustration and despair can result from experiences where ideas are misunderstood, actions are partially or even wholly unsuccessful, or politics reveal their limitations. Yet each time a failure was shared, it was not framed as an end point but as a moment in which new directions, questions, strategies, and spaces might appear. Rather than leading to paralysis, these "defeats" were recast as opportunities.

These moments of blockage and growth relate to both language and action—our frames for understanding and changing the world. Gayatri Chakravorty Spivak shared challenges relating to how her work on "subalternity" has traveled, particularly in the translation of ideas to categories that are materially and politically useful:

> "Can the Subaltern Speak?" was really a beginning, and then things changed. . . . When the rights of citizenship cannot be accessed, as in the case of Palestine, that is certainly subalternity. . . . And when our Palestinian colleagues suffer absolute discrimination in international professional travel, that is subalternization. Subalternity and subalternization are two different things, again asking for different kinds of strategies. . . . We certainly need to engage with them—not just to learn from them how to teach, but also to consolidate infrastructure so that someday they can be heard.
>
> If you just keep it as an idea, or especially if people come forward and say, "I'm a subaltern, I can speak. Hey, listen!"

they haven't understood that it's not about self-promotion. Not every kind of suffering or location is subalternity as one can use it. . . . Someone asked me, "How can you do it?" I can't tell you. I'm just failing. I've learned for thirty-six years. Because you don't undo the denial of intellectual labor—which is another condition of subalternity—by just being nice. I'm learning how to learn from failures and not think of them as failures.

Rather than descend into an academic debate that guards the territory of what subalternity *is*, Spivak reorients the discussion toward what subalternity *can do* if taken up as originally formulated. Failure becomes a commitment to learning.

The question of *how to do it*—utility and strategy—was picked up by Mustafa Barghouti, whom Ilan invited to speak precisely to the question of failure in their conversation about "the left." For Barghouti, the standards against which success and failure are measured must be reevaluated by expanding our field of view:

The question about failure must be addressed from three different angles: the global context, the regional context, and then the Palestinian internal context. Globally speaking, we know that capitalism has been hugely successful and actually morphed into new forms, including neoliberalism and what I call "global colonialism." . . . We [also] know that there are counter-democratic and counterrevolutionary forces that are against liberation and against democratization of the region. . . . [W]hen we talk about the Palestinian context, and that's the third aspect, one has to look at certain factors which have affected classical left parties in Palestine, weakening and marginalizing them to a large extent.

The "failure" of the left in Palestine cannot be isolated from global and regional contexts in which capitalism, colonialism, and counterrevolution articulate together—we are reminded to question *how things work*. While the result of this alignment of power across scales appears to be the foreclosure of liberation or democratization, Barghouti stops short of accepting failure as absolute. Instead, he directs our attention to what might emerge when "success" is seemingly delayed or thwarted:

> One has to see a new question that the failures probably are creating new opportunities, creating new spaces. But the failure here is not related to the left only. It is also related to the failure of those reactionary groups that took over in solving the economic and social problems. That combination is creating space for change, globally and locally.

Perhaps the lesson here is that failure is seldom what it seems to be, though we must never dismiss the costs and effects when ideas and actions fall short: economic crisis, viral pandemic, climate catastrophe, and genocide, at the extreme. Like Spivak and Barghouti, movements for decolonization can hold these things to be true and at the same time find value in questioning whether failure signals simply an ending. In doing so, we make space for the possibility that "under certain circumstances failing, losing, forgetting, unmaking, undoing, unbecoming, not knowing may in fact offer more creative, more cooperative, more surprising ways of being in the world."[14]

Sixth Lesson: Engage with/in the Arts

This volume draws together the work and words of esteemed intellectuals, many of whom contribute to material decolonization by using their public and institutional platforms in the service of movements for justice and liberation. Yet a subtle current ran beneath our conversations, at times gently breaking the surface to urge us to reflect on how people are reached and moved to join us. As academics and editors, it is uncomfortable to admit that sometimes the language of concepts, theories, policies, and law fails. When this happens, which means of communication rise to carry the work of agitating, educating, and organizing? What might have always already been there, telling the story and building solidarity better than we could hope to?

Our clearest voices belong to artists, poets, and writers—those for whom reality and imagination exist in generative, often intimate, relation. As made visible within our first lesson from the conversation series ("Learn your history"), the intellectual life of a people or place emerges not solely through academic labor and institutionalization. Rather its fullness is expressed through memory, embodiment, sensation, emotion, and even dreams. These forms of knowledge are crucial to political and intellectual consciousness, as Paul Gilroy relayed in a personal story:

> In my own life, the invasion of Lebanon in the early 1980s was a very important and formative experience for me. . . . And here, my teacher was the African American poet and writer June Jordan. She was the person who instructed me, informed me, and educated me as to how that concern, that openness, that attachment to the struggles of Palestinian people could be interwoven, interlaced, or productively entangled with the kinds of things that were emerging in my own work at that point.

Gilroy pointed to Jordan's poem "Apologies to All the People in Lebanon"[15] as significant in helping him to develop the ability to connect his work on racism and racialization in Britain with Palestine and the lives of Palestinians. Poetry elicited "concern," "openness," and "attachment" in a way that aligned knowledge across contexts and communities.

Yet a poetic mode of expression is also valuable for how it leads us toward what is not yet known or cannot be fully grasped. Again, we turn to Gilroy's lived experience:

> Like June Jordan, Ammiel Alcalay is a great and thoughtful poet. He's an extraordinary poet. So maybe there's something about poets in this who are able to do things that political theorists, philosophers, and historians aren't able to do. And that poetic payoff is something that we should try to study, because it seems to me that there's something about the way that language is being used. There's something about the way in which newness is being brought into the world in this very difficult and massively overdetermined area that suggests that poets are able to summon and conjure with words in ways that are extremely important.

The "payoff" of expression is not a single poem that might be read and shared, but the ways in which poetic language calls us to the world. Whether through poetry, literature, film, photography, or music, the arts open us up—we are made new to the world and to each other. The newness of which Gilroy speaks is not an ability to see differently, as if through a previously hidden or unknown lens; it is the entry of *something that has not been before*. A possibility, a future.

With this in mind we turn to Elias Khoury, a storyteller of the highest regard, to close our sixth and final lesson:

> You need a dream. You need a dream to write books. You need a dream to make a revolution. You need a dream to teach deep from your heart. Otherwise, it's meaningless. . . . We need a deep reconciliation of accepting the other and

trying to build a new democratic place—a place where our religious identity is not the dominant identity. The dominant identity is our human identity. This is how I dream.

And I think this is what gave me the potential to write a novel like *Children of the Ghetto*. This dream enabled me to go through this very dark history, which is as if you are going inside your dark selves—this is the heart of darkness. This is the real heart of darkness that literature can help us to understand. Not to solve, but to understand. How to solve it is up to the new generation, who must teach us.

FOR THE FUTURE

Our task now is to take these lessons forward, into our struggles and commitments. The conversations that unfold within these pages speak to the difficulty of the road ahead, just as they relentlessly imagine a future of justice, liberation, and self-determination—in Palestine and beyond. From settler-colonial violence and authoritarianism to climate change, health inequality, and food insecurity, researchers, educators, and organizers are doing the work of critical analysis. At the same time, this energy is oriented toward a material decolonial horizon. For some, the labor of prognosis—forecasting or anticipating—reveals a desire to help produce an antidote to the political disunity that pervades the Palestinian national movement. For others, their future work draws Palestine together with aligned struggles in which they are also active or invested—these visions move us toward a renewed sense of the international.

As the speakers in our series made knowable, the discipline of Palestine studies might be understood as a point of confluence: a place where streams meet and join, and from which they flow together as something greater. Our guests spoke to how Indigenous studies, literature, social psychology, economics, international law, transnationalism, settler-colonial studies, and cultural studies offer theoretical nuance, comparative or parallel case studies, and strategies for resistance and organizing. Yet despite clear rigor and innovation, the pursuit of knowledge through activism-engaged scholarship is met with a special kind of vehemence, particularly when it comes to Palestine. In Britain, the Prevent program is increasingly mobilized to silence debates and research on Palestine. Developed as a counterterrorism initiative that identifies those most vulnerable "to being drawn into extremism" prior to radicalization,[16] Prevent empowers institutions and their employees to provide the police with information about activities, ideas, and identities. A similar attempt at regulation can be seen in the equation of criticism of Israel with Holocaust denial, made possible through the International Holocaust Remembrance Alliance definition.[17] Its widespread adoption among institutions, from states to universities, threatens to silence and punish those who question Israel's narrative and actions.

While the degree of coordination vis-à-vis Palestine is noteworthy, the force of reaction is not dissimilar to that previously unleashed on anticolonial struggles such as the Front de Libération Nationale (FLN) in Algeria, the Mau Mau in Kenya, the National Liberation Front of South Vietnam (or Viet Cong) in Vietnam, or other liberation movements deemed "terrorist organizations" by those in positions of power. However, Noam Chomsky offered a surprisingly optimistic reading of recent attempts at suppression:

> I think the increase in intensity of efforts to silence discussion on this topic is a sign of increased desperation among supporters of Israeli policy. As they see the control of opinion slipping

out of their hands, they're resorting to harsher and more desperate measures to try to block any discussion, any condemnation. In a way, it's sort of a good sign to see the extremism of attempts to silence discussion—it means the situation is getting out of their control.

In these moments, we must remember precisely what we pledge when aspiring or claiming to be committed thinkers, scholars, and activists. Faced with increasingly desperate and sometimes violent measures as control begins to slip, we must continue to challenge dehumanization in all its forms—wherever it arises. This commitment is the basis of an old/new form of solidarity. We turn once again to Angela Y. Davis:

> Solidarity is especially important for people who are engaged in struggle in the US. Because Black people, for example, have always been the recipients of solidarity from the era of slavery—when Frederick Douglass traveled to Ireland and Scotland, and when Ida B. Wells got support during her travels abroad in organizing the anti-lynching movement. That has become an instinct—for the world to pay attention to Black struggles in the US.
>
> We forget that as we have been recipients of solidarity over the years, decades and centuries, we also need to learn how to generate solidarity with people who are struggling in other parts of the world. This is central for the continued progressive radical development of the antiracist movement in the US. And it's important for us to make connections with struggles against settler colonialism. The US is a settler-colonial country, and therefore we can learn a great deal from Palestinians' struggles against settler colonialism. And from recognizing that Palestine is still subject to

that process—Israel is the only settler-colonial nation that continues to try to expand.

During this period when technology creates possibilities of communicating across national borders, we need to share with each other, learn from each other, and figure out how we might begin to create global movements. This will require us to try to popularize analyses of the role that global capitalism plays today; it will also require us to share different feminist approaches. Ultimately, I think we all want a world in which national boundaries do not define relationships among human beings—we want to try to imagine new modes of community that do not depend on the idea of the nation, which is a production of capitalism. So, I'm going to use the old term "international solidarity" because I think it still really resonates. We still need international solidarity.[18]

This is the future to which we devote our intellectual vision, our political will, and our material labor. Working toward decolonization entails a commitment to constant education—to learning our histories, developing new languages, and questioning *how things work*. It also means engaging with the aspects of transformation that are less readily grasped, from emotion and sensation to failure and artistic expression. These lessons become tools with which we tell stories of struggle and community, tales of the worlds we are actively building. *Palestine in a World on Fire* offers our belief that words, stories, and dialogue can play a role, modest as it might be, in creating a future where knowledge does not fan the flames of injustice and devastation—but serves the aims of justice and liberation.

THE CONVERSATIONS

Mustafa Barghouti

LIBERATION AND THE LEFT

January 20, 2022

Mustafa Barghouti is a prominent politician, campaigner, and physician with a long history of organizing and advocacy in Palestine. He is the leader of the Palestinian National Initiative (PNI), or al-Mubadara, a democratic movement that provides an alternative to Fatah and Hamas as dominant political parties. In 2005 Barghouti ran as the PNI's candidate for the presidential election, coming in second to Mahmoud Abbas. In 2006 he was elected as a member of the Palestinian parliament, and he served as former minister of information under the 2007 National Unity Government. In 2010 Barghouti was nominated for the Nobel Peace Prize, in recognition of his social, political, human rights, and peace activism. He is one of the most active grassroots leaders in Palestine, campaigning for the development of Palestinian civil society and grassroots democracy while advocating for internal reform. Dr. Barghouti is an international spokesperson for the Palestinian cause, a leading figure in the nonviolent popular resistance against the occupation and apartheid, and an organizer of the international solidarity presence

33

in Palestine. He is the founder and president of the Palestinian Medical Relief Society and writes extensively for local and international audiences on civil society and democracy issues and the political situation in Palestine, as well as on health development policy in Palestine. He recently published *The Ploy of the Century: Dimensions and Confrontational Strategies* (Centre for Arab Unity Studies, 2020).

ILAN PAPPÉ: Dear Mustafa, let us start with some historical questions that are relevant to the present. Your personal biography and that of the Arab left are intertwined in many ways and lead me to think about your recent political house, the Palestinian National Initiative, and the situation of the Palestinian left in our times. You grew up surrounded by internationalist ideas, in a family committed to struggle against national and social injustices, which explains why in a certain moment in your life you were also a member of the Palestinian People's Party (the former communist party of Palestine), as I was in its parallel sister party inside Israel.

In our institute and with colleagues from around the world, we have revisited the failures and achievements of the Arab left in the past, and wondered about the possible role the left, and in particular the Arab and Palestinian left, can play in our times in struggles— such as the struggle for the liberation of Palestine. I would like to ask if there is still a left and does it have a role in the liberation struggle?

A follow-up question is whether the Palestinian National Initiative, or al-Mubadara, which you established together with the late Edward Said, the late Haidar Abdel-Shaf'i, and others, is part of this new left? Does it create a new language for the left? Does it create a new kind of activism, which is different from the way organizations like this behaved in the past?

Does it have a special role to play? Particularly as we know how Israeli settler colonialism is intertwined with neoliberalism, as you warned us when writing about the ways that neocapitalist states deal with the question of refugees and immigrants in this century.

MUSTAFA BARGHOUTI: Let me start by talking about whether there is a role for the left. Of course—there is no doubt about that. Can there be a future role? Absolutely. That's the short answer, but the question about failure must be addressed from three different angles: the global context, the regional context, and then the Palestinian internal context. Globally speaking, we know that capitalism has been hugely successful and actually morphed into new forms, including neoliberalism and what I call "global colonialism." By that, I mean that class division is happening now, not only at the level of each country, but at the global level itself. To the extent that there are "exploiting" countries and "exploited" countries. That is a very important change and it has affected the ability of many left movements to be effective, including in Palestine and the Arab world.

The second context, which is very important now in the Arab region, is the regional one. We know that there are counter-democratic and counterrevolutionary forces that are against liberation and against democratization of the region. And I would say that these are movements, these are countries, and on top of them is Israel. In my opinion, the Zionist establishment is doing everything it can to prevent Arab countries from transforming into a democratic system. They are against democratization of the Palestinian infrastructure. Add to that the reactionary Arab regimes, the effect of the so-called petrodollar and its funding of counterrevolutions—this has definitely affected the possibility of democratic and left transformations in the region.

At the same time, one has to see a new question that the failures probably are creating new opportunities, creating new spaces. But the failure here is not related to the left only. It is also related to the failure of those reactionary groups that took over in solving the economic and social problems. That combination is creating space for change, globally and locally. We see interesting developments in Chile. We see the rise of Black Lives Matter in the United States. We see a serious movement against this horrible regime in Brazil. And here in the Arab world, I encourage everyone to keep following what's happening today in Tunisia and Sudan, which sounds like the renovation of the Arab democratic revolutions. I think the left there is already playing a very important role.

What is different about the Palestinian National Initiative and about many other new movements is that they are more flexible and less dogmatic than the previous forms of the left. That gives them the ability to be more effective. But when we talk about the Palestinian context, and that's the third aspect, one has to look at certain factors which have affected classical left parties in Palestine, weakening and marginalizing them to a large extent.

I would say that there are three factors here. The first factor is that some of these parties were too dependent on the Soviet Union—and when the Soviet Union collapsed, they were dramatically affected. The second factor was the lack of understanding in some of these parties of the value and importance of democracy and internal democracy. But also the inability to deal with the national question—sometimes mistakes were made, and that weakened the left parties. The inability to deal with religious societies and the question of how to approach religion in this context also had a great impact.

These factors have all affected and are related to weakening some of these groups. But the most important factor in the Palestinian context for me today, and maybe this is what distinguishes the Palestinian Initiative from other left parties, is that some parties were unable to be independent—independent in their vision, independent in their program, and independent in their practice. And some are too attached to one of the two main streams in Palestinian society: Fatah and Hamas.

In the Palestinian National Initiative, we believe that you cannot really be effective unless you create an independent program, an independent vision, and an independent practice from these two parties. In doing so, one can try to represent what I call "the silent majority" in Palestinian society. That's what we saw, for instance, during the Palestinian presidential elections in 2005—a huge power is waiting and looking for an alternative. Some left parties only have the name of the left and they are unable to create that space of independence, which makes them vulnerable to being controlled by right-wing parties, conservative parties. And the question of alliances, with whom do they ally in elections, is a very interesting and indicative one.

Is al-Mubadara different from that? I believe so. It's trying to be different, and here the name is not as important as the substance—you can call it a democratic left tendency or an independent one. But the most important distinguishing characteristics are, first, independence from the two major streams in the Palestinian society, as I said. Second, the initiative is in opposition to the system of nepotism and clientelism that sometimes dominates political life. Third, it concentrates not only on the issue of national struggle and liberation from Israeli occupation and the system of apartheid, but also it focuses on social justice: workers' rights, poor people's rights, marginalized groups, women's rights. And it also relates to youth—around 85 percent of its membership are young people and women.

But one of the most important things is the issue of democracy. There is no compromise about freedom of speech, about the separation of powers, about fighting authoritarianism internally in Palestine. And the activism here is related to struggling for internal freedom as well. Finally, I would say that this movement has had three avant-garde positions or activities that made it different. One is its practical involvement in popular resistance. Second, its involvement in the Boycott, Divestment, Sanctions (BDS) campaign. Third, its emphasis that we are not fighting only to end occupation, but to end the system of apartheid and discrimination in historic Palestine.

ILAN PAPPÉ: I would like to talk about the Palestinian political reality and the Palestinian national movement in a wider context, not just in the occupied territories. Like so many of us, you were impressed by the eleven days of resistance we witnessed throughout historic Palestine in May 2021.[1] Can this unity on the ground be a factor encouraging unity from above, so to speak? Quite a few activists suggested even before those events that there is a need for fundamental change in the liberation movement as a whole. Some suggested either restructuring the PLO and making it a more representative body, or even creating together a new outfit that will integrate the various Palestinian movements and orientate the struggle in the future. Something that represents not only Palestinians in the West Bank and the Gaza Strip, Palestinian society, wherever it exists. What is your response to these initiatives? Do you think they are relevant, important, or vital? Or is now not the time to consider such initiatives, and leave the political structures more or less as they are?

MUSTAFA BARGHOUTI: What happened in May was a turning point. In the sense of the unity among Palestinians, it was a really unifying moment—between Palestinians in the occupied territories, those who live in Israel, and those who live in the diaspora. I always say that the struggle against oppression unifies us, while the struggle for authority divides us. Unfortunately, the struggle for authority in Palestine is about an authority that is totally under Israeli military occupation. So, what happened in May had an impact and will continue to have an impact. But this unity on the ground, at the grassroots level, is not yet reflected at the level above. We see an objective need, an objective reality, that requires unity among Palestinians, but at the same time we see a different line being followed.

In reality, what we see is that the Oslo process and Oslo agreement have divided the Palestinians into those who are in the occupied territories, those who are in 1948 areas, and those who are in the diaspora and felt left out. Occupation transformed into apartheid or actually ethnic cleansing, which was very well described in the Human Rights Watch report, and the B'Tselem report, and previously the Economic and Social Commission for Western Asia (ESCWA) report that was never adopted by the United Nations. All these reports have shown that the system of oppression is unifying Palestinians, because it affects all three parts at the same time. And in my opinion, and the opinion of the Palestinian Initiative, the central goal of the Palestinian liberation movement needs to change.

It cannot continue to say that our goal is to end occupation only. It has to say that our goal is to end occupation and to bring down the system of oppressive, racist apartheid in all of Palestine. I don't see a difference between what's happening today in the Negev, in terms of the uprising there, and what's happening among the Palestinians in Lod, or in Burqa or Beita in the West Bank, or Jerusalem or Hebron. It's the same struggle against the same enemy, and the same form of oppression. And that's why today we need a new form of unity. I don't know what this form will take, but I know that there is an objective need for a system that unifies the struggle of Palestinians in all these areas.

To achieve that, I believe four preconditions are required quickly. The first is that the Palestinian leadership must adopt an alternative program of struggle, an alternative to the Oslo approach, an alternative to this myth of the possibility of compromise. Second, there must be acceptance of the idea of participatory democracy, or unity that is based on the democratic participation of people. Third, there must be the right of Palestinians to elect their representatives. We have been denied this right. We haven't had any elections since 2006. And the people have the right to choose their leaders, specifically for the Palestinian National Council, which is the parliament or the governing body of the PLO. We need to find forms to unify the struggle of Palestinians in a more effective way.

About the PLO: I totally support the need for a democratic restructuring of the PLO, which is the only way to bring back its very vital role. The PLO has been co-opted by the Palestinian Authority (PA). It is crippled. It has lost the ability to be influential, and that is a big challenge facing the Palestinians. But at the same time, we must balance between two things: true democratic representation of the Palestinian people in their leadership structure and sustaining the right of Palestinians to represent themselves. That's why the PLO is important—because it is recognized as a representative of the Palestinian people internationally and at the level of the Arab world.

We all know that one of the goals of "the deal of the century" by President Trump—which was written by Netanyahu rather than Trump, in my opinion—was eliminating the right of the Palestinian people to represent themselves. And that's what this Israeli government is trying to do. They want to discuss our issues with those countries that are normalizing relations with the Israeli occupation. And that's why, while maintaining our right to represent ourselves by sustaining the role of the PLO is an important goal, the PLO itself must change and be democratically restructured. There are many new initiatives in Palestine. The PNI are the only movement that joined the PLO, was allowed into the PLO, or managed to enter the PLO after waiting for ten years. But there are many new movements in Palestine, and these people should be given the chance to be represented through democratic elections.

ILAN PAPPÉ: Yes, let's move to the international arena. Because even if we know that efforts for unity and more democratic representation are successful, a lot of what happens in Palestine, and will occur in Palestine, also depends on the international community. In her excellent book, *A History of False Hope*, Lori Allen describes various junctures in which the international community pretended to investigate the violations of Palestinian rights, without any real intention or willingness to confront Israel and its exceptional immunity in the international community. She mentions the term "democratic listeners." For those of us who might think that the problem was only Trump, all prior American administrations followed a very similar line. Democratic listening is a futile act of sympathy with the Palestinians by people such as the former president Barack Obama. Unfortunately, I think this will be true of Joe Biden as well.

And I thought of something you commented on when Barack Obama came to the occupied territories and stated that he came "to listen." You reacted by saying, "We Palestinians have been listening for too long. This passivity on Obama's part is unacceptable and dangerous."

This leads me to the question of Israel's exceptionalism. Have we become better in dealing with Israel's exceptional immunity from international intervention and rebuke? And is this something you think that academic communities can contribute to in this regard? Because this exceptionalism is the shield of immunity that prevents governments in the West, and beyond, from taking any action in support and solidarity with the Palestinians.

MUSTAFA BARGHOUTI: The short answer to your question is, not yet. We haven't yet become better. And before I explain, I would like to remind everyone that what you said is that really what we need is a new understanding of the relationship between settler colonialism and the system of apartheid with global neocapitalism. Academics have the duty of trying to explain why all the right-wingers, the extreme fascists, and the reactionaries in so many countries support Israeli policy. What is the connection? Why is Bolsonaro such a supporter of Israel? Why is Trump such a supporter of this Israeli government and its policies? Why are the racists in Hungary and Austria doing the same? Why is Israel creating alliances, even security and military alliances, with the most reactionary Arab regimes?

It's very clear that there is a real connection with settler colonialism, which sees itself as an extension of other settler colonialisms in other places. That's why I believe that the entry point to explaining the Palestinian problem, and to building solidarity with Palestine, should be the criticism of apartheid and an explanation of what apartheid means in Palestine—and why the system is much worse than the apartheid that prevailed in South Africa. We must identify the challenges facing us, why we cannot yet overcome this system of impunity that Israel enjoys.

There are several challenges. One is the fact that Israel continues to use and abuse the relationship of the Holocaust with Israel. Second, Israel also uses the fact that it is a base for global colonialism today. This is the reason for the role it plays vis-à-vis the Gulf, other countries in the region, and the strategic balance in the Middle East. Third, we are facing one of the most developed and the most organized lobbies in the world. Finally, it is important to emphasize that Israel is using what I call "intellectual terrorism" or "mental terrorism"—a strategy of frightening people. Anyone who struggles against Israeli occupation is described as a terrorist.

If you use the most nonviolent form of resistance, you are called a violent person. If you resist occupation by speaking against it, you are described as a provocateur. And if you are supporting Palestinians, they describe you as antisemitic. And people like you, Ilan, will be described as self-hating Jews. There is a whole system that attempts to frighten people and prevent them from expressing their opinions.

Recently we have witnessed a very sharp increase in these attacks. First, the attack on BDS, which you can see in Britain, France, and the United States. There are even laws against BDS. There are also the three most dangerous instruments that are used against solidarity with Palestinians and Palestinian society: NGO Monitor, UK lawyers, and UN Watch. These three instruments are mobilized specifically to attack Palestinian civil society.

And why are they attacking the most developed civil society in the Arab world? Because they want to deprive Palestinians of the role that civil society organizations play in supporting the steadfastness of the Palestinian people. Second, to prevent their role in exposing the human rights violations that Israel commits. And third, to prevent civil society organizations from playing a very important role in trying to introduce democracy in Palestine. In that sense, what we witness here is a very dangerous effort to dehumanize the Palestinian struggle.

Of course, there are successes—I admire actions by people like Susan Sarandon and Emma Watson, who broke the wall of fear. And the role you play, Ilan, along with Noam Chomsky, Daniel Barenboim, and others. We also see a change in the Democratic Party in the United States, especially among young people. I do believe that academics have a role to play here.

But there are two very important conditions if we want to succeed. The first is not to be defensive, to take the initiative. If we are defensive, we will always lose the fight. And second, to organize. The more we can organize to counter these lobbies, the more we can succeed in bringing down Israel's impunity.

ILAN PAPPÉ: You mentioned what's going on today in the Negev. I don't think many people outside historic Palestine know about it, because I haven't seen any reports in Western media about how the Palestinians of the south have taken action against an insidious Israeli plan to plant European pine tree forests in the desert. For some reason, Israelis feel intimidated by the desert and they want to turn it into a European forest. But of course, the main objective of that forestation project is to try to squeeze the Palestinians in the south into an enclave that would prevent them from developing their economy, social cohesion, and national aspiration.

This brings me to the question of decolonization that you've already touched upon. One of the important networks supporting this series is the Exeter Decolonizing Network, which indeed sees colonization as prevailing in many parts in the world, including the West. We have moved quite far with our deliberations on the question of decolonization in our times. It is clear that decolonization is a relevant process for our century and for all our societies, and particularly for Palestine. What I really like about your work, Mustafa, is its clarity; you unpack clearly what decolonization means when talking about the liberation of Palestine. Before talking about the possible endgame of this process, namely how we should imagine a decolonized historic Palestine, I would like to go back to the modes of Palestinian resistance. Some of them you mentioned, like BDS and steadfastness, or *sumud*—but there is also popular resistance on the ground.

We saw it in the Great March of Return in Gaza and we see it now in the Naqab, which succeeded at least temporarily in stopping the forestation project.[2] And we see it in East Jerusalem where we were less successful against the ethnic cleansing that is taking place. Is something missing in this resistance on the ground that people should know and understand? Because the Israelis also like to convey the message of Palestinians' passivity, of acceptance or resignation, and therefore claim there's no need for any dramatic change in the status quo. But those of us who are on the ground know that the resistance of individuals and collectives is still happening. Can you see something like a third uprising, a third intifada, being part of that resistance in the future?

MUSTAFA BARGHOUTI: I do see that, yes. I don't know when and I don't know exactly which form it will take, but since 2015 we've been moving in that direction. Specifically, since the people of Palestine are almost 100 percent convinced that the Oslo path has failed, that the Palestinian Authority has failed, that this reliance on the compromise with Israel is not working, they are seeking ways to struggle back. And I believe that many of the new forms have been used before. This popular resistance is the new form of struggle in Palestine, which does not negate the right of Palestinians to use all other forms of resistance, as long as they respect international law.

Palestinians in Gaza frequently use military struggle to defend themselves, to deter Israeli aggression. That is well known. But the most popular and effective form of resistance is what we've been advocating: popular resistance. As we invent and use new forms, we are in a dynamic process—because the establishment constantly tries to co-opt and neutralize these forms, to make them an official ministry or a governmental body. But it is not working. I want people to understand that this is a dynamic process—it's not just a new form that you discover and use. You first struggle on the ground to promote these forms.

I would add to popular resistance the issue of steadfastness. In the '70s and '80s, this was the main goal: how to help people remain steadfast against occupation. This is becoming even more important today. Because it is the main instrument to prevent ethnic cleansing in many areas, especially in Area C, which represents 62 percent of the West Bank. So many communities like Sheikh Jarrah, Khan al-Ahmar, and the Negev in the south of historic Palestine are being subjected to ethnic cleansing. BDS is another very important form of resistance. It translates solidarity with Palestinians into material power—into an economic effect that impacts occupation. It also provides Palestinians in the diaspora with an effective form of participating in the struggle of their people.

Popular resistance, or nonviolent resistance, is not passive resistance. On the contrary, it will become the most important form of struggle against apartheid. Our goal in the struggle is to change the balance of power, to fix the severe disparity between Palestinians and the Israeli establishment. We speak about six pillars of struggle as a strategy: popular resistance; BDS; steadfastness; integrating the struggle between Palestinians in the occupied territories, in 1948 areas, and in the diaspora; and the creation of a unified democratic leadership. We need that desperately as a way to achieve national unity. Finally, the sixth pillar is the penetration of the circles of our opponents and working with different groups to mobilize solidarity with the Palestinian cause.

ILAN PAPPÉ: You defined your and the PNI's vision for the future as including, among other aspirations, the following: "Bringing an end to the system of apartheid in all parts of historic Palestine." Does this mean the establishment of a single democratic state? Is such a project plausible? More generally, how do you imagine a decolonized Palestine, if all the struggles you describe would be successful, if we succeed in galvanizing the international community, and if we can change the balance of power? Is this something that is part of your vision or are you strategically focusing on a very near future, rather than a more distant one?

MUSTAFA BARGHOUTI: This is a very good question. I believe that bringing down the system of apartheid in all parts of historic Palestine could mean one democratic state, yes. Theoretically, there is no problem with that. Practically, we need to be careful about not engaging on this level at this time and creating a new division between Palestinians—between those who want an independent Palestinian state and those who favor one democratic state. So while I say that one democratic state, which was the original Palestinian goal, would be the right concept, our new program concentrates on ending the system of apartheid in all of Palestine, including ethnic cleansing and occupation. But also exercising the right of Palestinians of self-determination. The right of self-determination means that I am not the one who will decide the form that Palestinians will choose, but it's all of us as Palestinians.

Let me also say here that, logically speaking, one democratic state is the right approach. But there will never be one democratic state, or an independent Palestinian state in the West Bank and Gaza, without bringing down apartheid. We often hear counterarguments from people who say that Israel will never accept a one-state solution. My response to them is usually: Does Israel accept a two-state solution anyhow? Of course not. They do not accept a two-state solution or a one-state solution. We need to understand the reality that we live in today. And the reality is that we already live in one state, but with a system of apartheid. That's what I wish every diplomat in this world would understand, especially diplomats in Europe. We already live in one apartheid state. That is the reality of today.

And that is why bringing down apartheid is the most important issue. It is one apartheid state with a process of gradual, continuous annexation of the West Bank, piece by piece. We want to break down apartheid, and I don't care if this Israeli establishment accepts or does not accept that. I would ask the question, when did liberation movements decide their goal based on what their colonizers would accept? Is that what Algeria did when it struggled for independence? Is that what South Africans did when they struggled against apartheid? Is that what Vietnam did when it struggled for its freedom? No. And in my opinion, the sin of the PLO leadership at the time was accepting to make its goal a negotiated agreement.

A negotiated solution meant that the international community gave Israel the right to veto the establishment of an independent Palestinian state and ending the occupation. Otherwise, why would all these European countries that speak about a two-state solution still abstain from recognizing the Palestinian state while they recognize Israel?

I would also warn against one specific thing, which is that we need to be very careful with those who say that there is no possibility for a two-state solution *without* saying, "What is the alternative?" These people are practically supporters of the Israeli establishment and the status quo—of keeping the system of apartheid. We need to differentiate this camp from the camp that you represent, or the camp that I represent, in struggling against apartheid. It is our duty to explain to our friends that the status quo cannot be maintained. I listen to diplomats who support two-state solutions, but they keep saying that we need to stabilize the situation. Their goal as diplomats is to stabilize the status quo. My goal is to destabilize the status quo, and it should be our goal to destabilize the status quo and change it. Because that's the only way to get to freedom and to decolonize this horrible system.

Judith Butler

ON HUMANITY, VIOLENCE, AND IMAGINATION

April 29, 2021

Judith Butler is Distinguished Professor in the Graduate School at the University of California, Berkeley, where they have taught in Critical Theory and Comparative Literature for several years. They received their PhD in Philosophy from Yale University in 1984. They are the author of several books, including *Subjects of Desire: Hegelian Reflections in Twentieth-Century France* (1987), *Gender Trouble: Feminism and the Subversion of Identity* (1990), *Bodies That Matter: On the Discursive Limits of "Sex"* (1993), *The Psychic Life of Power: Theories of Subjection* (1997), *Excitable Speech* (1997), *Antigone's Claim: Kinship Between Life and Death* (2000), *Precarious Life: Powers of Violence and Mourning* (2004), *Frames of War: When Is Life Grievable?* (2009), *Parting Ways: Jewishness and the Critique of Zionism* (2012), *Who Sings the Nation-State?* with Gayatri Chakravorty Spivak (2008), *Dispossession: The Performative in the Political* coauthored with Athena Athanasiou (2013), *Notes Toward a Performative Theory of Assembly* (2015), *Vulnerability in Resistance* coauthored with

Zeynep Gambetti and Leticia Sabsay (2016), *The Force of Non-Violence* (2020), and *What World Is This? A Pandemic Phenomenology* (2022). Butler's books have been translated into more than twenty-seven languages, and they have received fourteen honorary degrees. They were, from 2015 to 2020, a principal investigator of the Mellon Foundation Grant that initiated the International Consortium of Critical Theory Programs on whose board they now serve as cochair. Butler is active in several human rights organizations, having served on the board of the Center for Constitutional Rights in New York and presently participating on the advisory board of Jewish Voice for Peace. They also serve on the boards of several journals, including *Critical Times*. They were the recipient of the Andrew Mellon Award for Distinguished Academic Achievement in the Humanities (2009–13). Butler was elected to the British Academy as a Corresponding Fellow in 2018 and to the American Academy of Arts and Sciences in 2019. In 2020, they served as president of the Modern Language Association. They were a visiting scholar at the Centre Pompidou in 2023 through 2024. In 2024, they published *Who's Afraid of Gender?* with Farrar, Straus, and Giroux.

ILAN PAPPÉ: Judith, these questions stem directly from what we've heard from you over the years—from your books, articles, lectures, and interviews. And this imparts a logic that connects our subjects of interest, from attitudes toward life to the struggle for decolonization in the twenty-first century.

My first question is about the way we can operationalize your notions of the grievable and ungrievable in daily life experience. Not only in the questions of whose life is valuable, but rather in the field of compassion. Much of my effort, and that of many of my Palestinian friends who live in Israel, is focused on an attempt to engage the Jewish public there and in the world with the human

cost of the Palestinian 1948 catastrophe, the Nakba, which is com-
memorated every May 15th.

The effort here is to persuade them to acknowledge the Nakba
as a formative, recurring event that requires psychological, legal,
moral, and political closure. And to do it by showing basic compassion or grief toward the suffering of the victims of the Nakba, before
discussing anything else. When you try to do this, you are immediately faced with a callous wall of rejection, informed by a gut mechanism of defense that blocks any compassion. There is no grieving
for the Palestinian victims of the 1948 ethnic cleansing, as there
was no grieving or compassion toward the victims of Gaza in 2014.
This mechanism appears as a strange sequence of counterarguments
beginning with total denial of the catastrophe, followed by a statement that if it did happen the victims are responsible for their fate.
And finally, they would say that worse things happen elsewhere.

For me, this mechanism of defense is directly associated with
two examples of structural dehumanization: anti-Black racialized
violence in the US, epitomized by the murder of George Floyd and
others, and the dehumanization of the Palestinians. In many ways,
the interconnection between racism in the US and in Israel has
been recently recognized by the clear pro-Palestinian position of
the Black Lives Matter movement and by Palestinians in the Gaza
Strip, who demonstrated in solidarity with the victims of the police
violence in Ferguson.

Struggling against both forms of dehumanization can potentially be defined as part of the new decolonization effort—one that
will be effective only if it overcomes this dehumanization. How
could we best challenge dehumanization and the lack of compassion? Here we are concerned with the Jewish Zionist and Israeli
attitude to Palestinian suffering due to the ongoing catastrophe,
and the long history and continued racialized dehumanization of

African Americans in the United States. Because if we do not, we accept the American political science assertion that conflicts or social "tensions" can only be managed and never solved.

Can we move beyond this grievable/ungrievable dichotomy in daily activism that aims to persuade people to acknowledge the suffering of others, as part of a real effort to bring peace and a solution to violence?

JUDITH BUTLER: Ilan, let me first say how much I have learned from you over the years. You were among the first historians from within Israel who allowed me to reconstruct the history of the Nakba and also to see how systemic the denial of that catastrophe is in the official and unofficial Israeli narratives of the founding of the state of Israel. Your historical work and your conceptual work have very clearly paved the way for many of us, especially those of us who grew up within the matrix of Zionism for whom that was a worldview—a framework that was not exactly contestable as a young person. We didn't have an "outside" to that framework until the excellent work of historians and political activists started to open that up.

But over time, it's also been clear to me that the internal critique of the Nakba and the systematic dispossession of Palestinians from their lands—the dispossession, the incarceration, the killing, the siege, the forced exile—all of this requires a different set of histories than one that is simply the internal critique of Zionism that progressive or anti-Zionist Jews conduct. It's extremely important to develop this critique, except if we remain caught in that framework we're just talking to ourselves.

So part of me thinks well, yes, it's important to persuade Zionists within Israel or Zionists within the diaspora to understand the radical oppression of Palestine that not only happened in 1948 but continues to happen. The Nakba is indeed a continuing practice and policy—in occupation, in forced dispossession, in disenfranchisement, in Palestine and beyond. It has been important to leave that framework and to ask a different question: how to build international alliances that have, as a primary goal, the liberation of Palestine and the enfranchisement of Palestinians. And to recognize the condition under which Palestinians live, not only as settler colonial, but also as systemic racism.

As we do that, we link Palestine to other struggles, including the antiracism struggle in this country and throughout the world, but also prison abolition and carceral politics. If we think about the industries that have built the checkpoints and militarized police practices of the Israeli regime, they are very often the same corporations and practices that took place in Ferguson. And that take place in police trainings in Singapore, South Africa, and the United States. We have a global condition, which is the militarization of the police. And we also have a framework: understanding carceral politics as involving not just the abolition of prisons, but the prison system, as it extends into everyday life through the militarization of the police. That is already a framework that connects these struggles.

What you say about compassion is very important and I don't mean to set it aside. I sometimes worry about compassion, that it involves setting up identification: "These other people are just like me." Just as I suffer, so others suffer. Just as my people suffer, so others suffer. That is a principle of equality and it's an important one, but there's also a different history. If I really want to be affected by the catastrophe of the ongoing Nakba, if I want to make myself open to the suffering of others, it may be that I should not assume an absolute parallelism between the lives of others and my life. Because the tendency in the West is to say, "Oh, everyone is equal. Everyone is just like me, everyone is a Western subject." Through my compassion, which is very commendable, I assimilate everyone to me. And it's like, "No, that's not going to work because there's a separate history and it's one we need to learn."

It's also why many of us need to learn other languages, other histories, and other geographies—so that we don't assimilate the sufferings of others to our own suffering, because that just brings them into our model. Now we might say that this is a risk we take within the humanist perspective. And as you say, rightly, "How do we convince people, persuade people, or get them to understand this quite systematic dehumanization of Palestinians?" That's a perfectly great question. The problem I see is that there's an idea of the human that's lodged within the critique of dehumanization. If Palestinians or non-Palestinians want to say, "Palestinians are human just like everyone else," which version of the human are we invoking at that moment?

So it may be that we need a new global understanding of the human to move forward. I do think there's a hardness, a refusal to accept Palestinian suffering as suffering, on the part of those who want to give the state of Israel the right to enact every and any aggression in the name of self-defense. But cracking open that defensive, aggressive, murderous psychosocial position is an extremely difficult task. And my sense is that instead of persuading people one-on-one, we need to build the international alliance. To build a new consensus that Palestinian rights, Palestinian liberation, must be part of any left liberation struggle. And that a leftism that stops precisely at the moment of Palestine—"I'm left on all these positions, but not Palestine"—is an inconsistent and contradictory leftism.

I think we need to overwhelm them and surround them. We need to make this an unbeatable, un-overcome-able consensus, and we do that through knowledge, through media, through politics.

ILAN PAPPÉ: I still can't give up on hoping to penetrate through this world of dehumanization and rejection. But it is not the priority, I fully agree, and international networking is far more important. We need to prioritize some of our efforts.

My second question concerns gender, with specific interests stemming from our many colleagues and students who work on gender, sexuality, and feminisms—plural—in the Arab and Muslim world. My entry point is a short quotation from your work: "There is no gender identity behind the expressions of gender. That identity is performatively constituted by the very 'expressions' that are said to be its results." There are probably two ways to approach this question, a crude one and a more scholarly one. The cruder approach would be, what is the relevance of a movement such as #MeToo—born as a response to the general abuse of women and developed into a more high-profile exposure of certain misogynist and sexist work cultures in the Western media and entertainment workplace—to the struggle against a far harsher and at times far more brutal repression in the rest of the world?

Something was undoubtedly gained in the globalization of the movement—exposure, influence, and so on—but possibly other things were lost. For instance, an insistence on the centrality of race to the issue of gendered and sexualized violence. It feels like there are prospects for the movement's influence if these axes of difference are reengaged. Is this a case where universalism is actually Westernism? Or is it a case of an unrealized-as-yet universalism, as you put it when you expanded the meaning of universalism to include what has not yet been realized as universal, or is part of the promise of being universal? Put differently, what is your view on the scholarly and activist schism, or dispute, that unraveled between what we might call "Western feminisms," on the one hand, and Arab, Muslim, or Islamic feminisms—the ideas put forward by Amina Wadud, Leila Ahmed, and Fatema Mernissi—on the other?

Can there be a universal discussion on gender and sexuality that is blind to cultural context or cultural relativism?

JUDITH BUTLER: Well, I think there can be and in fact there is a global discussion on feminisms in the plural. But I'm not sure about universality. When we make universal claims, they always turn out to be parochial in some way—and they are always contested by what they exclude or what they efface. That means that when we seek to elaborate a general claim, we need to do it through the practice of translation. In other words, it is only through what Said, Spivak, and others have called "cultural translation" that we start to understand how something like the structural oppression of women throughout the globe takes place.

There's no single model that we can develop in one part of the world and impose upon the other. And, of course, I have emerged in the last thirty years through US feminism, which too often thought that feminist theory takes place in English. That whatever is said in English is therefore universally true! This elaborates a kind of cultural imperialism at the level of language, but even the term "gender" is not easily translatable. Many feminists have had to push back on the term gender, or to find innovations within their own languages because it doesn't fit with the syntax or perhaps it's not the central category for feminist concerns.

Gender Trouble, from which you cite, came out thirty-one years ago. It made general claims, but I don't think it sought to make universal claims. Its concern was precisely to see that the category of "woman" was assumed to have an integrity or foundational status that didn't work, that produced contestation. And I think we see that now as well, as trans women struggle to be recognized as women.

Is it possible to expand the category, to allow it a kind of historical elaboration or articulation, so that it becomes more inclusive? I wouldn't write *Gender Trouble* again, but one of the important perspectives that emerged from decolonial feminism is that colonial regimes instituted gender binaries as a Western imposition.

At the time, I just called it "the heterosexual matrix"—I don't think I would do that again. But the question of how that gender binary was instituted by colonial regimes is an extremely interesting one. There are many feminist scholars, in Uganda for instance, who are able to track the British imposition of the gender binary. We can certainly track the imposition of the French gender binary on its colonized spaces. So I think that a global feminism can take place, but not on the basis of assuming universality.

It worries me that in places like France, or in certain Anglo-American feminist circles, claims are made about feminism that presume that Islamic feminism or feminism that emerges from North Africa or the Middle East isn't "real feminism" because it doesn't have a Western idea of emancipation as its goal. For many years I've been appalled at how some self-proclaimed "feminists" in France, for instance, assume that all women who come from Arab or Islamic backgrounds in particular are subject to patriarchal control—and that nothing less than the destruction of the religion as a formative influence on women will liberate them. And this strikes me as an extraordinary form of Islamophobia that takes place under the name of feminism and is actively promoted through versions of European white feminism. That obviously needs to be dismantled. There's now extraordinary work that doesn't always get published or publicized in the American, British, and European academy from scholars like Leila Ahmed or Suad Joseph on the rich history and diversity of Islamic feminism. And even the convocations of Islamic feminism, one of which took place in France a couple of years ago. This was barely mentioned by the French press—as if it doesn't really exist, even though it had close to three thousand people attending.

So there's a cultural war going on. And if feminism is to be a progressive and emancipatory movement, it must be not only antiracist but also include in its antiracism an opposition to Islamophobia. And also other forms of racism against North African and Middle Eastern peoples that make the assumption that the Western ideal of feminism is the only possible emancipatory one. It's actually a form of cultural imperialism that traffics under the name of "emancipation." We all need to be involved in that criticism.

I think I'm known for the so-called performativity of gender thesis, and I will never live that down. It's only one part of my thinking and not one that I think about very much anymore in an active way—it's not the central aspect of my feminism. I draw from decolonial feminist work in Latin America, people like Rita Segato. I draw from Ni Una Menos, the wonderful movement in Argentina that has made waves throughout the world. I draw from the work of Françoise Vergès, Gayatri Spivak, Sara Ahmed, and my good friend Saba Mahmood who died a few years ago. I draw from a wide range of work now, and I think it's extremely interesting to think about what it takes to have a global conversation.

For me, the work of linguistic and cultural translation is key. We're constantly learning! Feminism has not just been about the equality of women, or the emancipation of women from violence and subordination. It has also been a question: What is it to be a woman, or how is that category built, regulated, or reproduced? And that means that the category is being rearticulated through time. If I were to revise the performativity thesis, I would say that we are still in the process of rearticulating the category of women, men, or other genders through different languages and different contexts. This historical renewability of these categories is crucial to our political discourse, and also part of the global challenge of feminism.

ILAN PAPPÉ: If we take the same question that we've just discussed and focus on the situation of LGBTQ communities in the Arab and Muslim world, I think it's more intricate or delicate. I remember joining a demonstration in Greece against the oppression of the Catholic minority by Orthodox Greek institutions with a friend who was part of the movement for civil rights there. He told me that in the evening he planned to demonstrate against the Catholic Church for its treatment of the queer and LGBT communities in Greece. It is very difficult indeed to navigate this particular matrix of the politics of identity in the Arab and Muslim world and remain a committed activist through performative action and resistance. And not succumb, for instance, to the defeatist Foucauldian view of the infinite power of repression, which you, among others, successfully challenged.

This challenge has never been more relevant than when discussing LGBTQ rights in the Arab and Muslim world. There are those, like Joseph Massad in his work, "The Gay International," who argue that in the past there were more discreet and pronounced ways of living LGBTQ lives that have now been substituted by more demonstrative ways of life and struggle imported from the West. These in turn produced existential dangers for the community that had not there before. I know this not just as an abstract idea. My friend Ussama Makdisi, in his recent book *Age of Coexistence: The Ecumenical Frame and the Making of the Modern Arab World*, speaks of an Arab world prior to imperialism, colonialism, and Zionism that did not insist on articulating and stressing every difference. Hence sectarianism was not a destructive phenomenon, but rather a delicate and at times haphazard way of living.

In a similar way, others argue that different gender identities were not insisted on but existed at that time. Do we again have a Western point of view masquerading as a universal one, devoid of historical and cultural context? Or do we need to be "glocal," at least on this issue, navigating between the principal and local realities? We're thinking here about the work by Jason Ritchie, "Black skin splits," and Rahul Rao's appeal in "Queer Questions" to employ what he called "heterotemporality": a situation in which "we could find a way to remain continuous with our past abjection without being traumatized by it." This "might keep us from descent into triumphalist futurity."

And if I just might add to this something else, a question that indicates that there is something positive in this delicate discussion. It's offered by Walaa Alqaisiya in her work on the Palestinian group alQaws for Sexual and Gender Diversity in Palestinian Society. Walaa argues that this is a productive site to think and practice decolonization, since it does not allow separating the struggle for gender rights from decolonization—and thus enables a very effective critique of Israel's pinkwashing.

Of course, alQaws is not the only place where pinkwashing is criticized, but it is important to hear it from within. So can we be more sanguine and, rather than aggravating the situation, use this particular topic to advance decolonization in Palestine and human rights elsewhere in the Arab world and beyond? I'm talking to you from Haifa today, and this topic is very difficult to engage with. But I think we need to continue engaging and perhaps find even better ways to bring the topic to the fore as part of a general discussion of human rights and decolonization.

JUDITH BUTLER: I used to meet with alQaws when I went to Palestine—I don't think I'm allowed through that border anymore. But my understanding in their writings, especially the work of Haneen Maikey and others, is that the struggle for LGBTQ rights must be linked with the critique of Zionism. And in particular the critique of settler colonialism as it has taken form and perpetuated itself in Palestine. That seems very clear and important. And one reason it's important is that it is not just a question of identity—meaning gay, lesbian, trans, bisexual identity and getting recognition *for identity*. "This is my identity. I want to be recognized and I don't want to be oppressed on the basis of my identity." These are also communities. These are networks, these are forms of life. And they're forms of life and communities that are figuring out how to live, how to support one another. And also how to be part of a larger struggle that opposes racism, settler colonialism, state violence, homophobia, transphobia, misogyny, and a whole list of interlocking oppressions.

On the one hand, yes, we want glocalism because we want to understand the very specific struggles that are taking place. Massad did make an important point, which is that hypervisibility is not always the main aim of LGBTQ movements outside the urban centers of Europe and the United States. The point is not to get more visibility, as if visibility itself were a good. Visibility also makes one a target. Visibility without a sustaining community and a neutralization of police violence or of social violence—visibilization does not achieve the goal. What one wants is visibility within a framework that is actually transforming society more broadly—not just on the issue of LGBTQI rights and emancipation, but on all of the interlocking issues. So we need to have an interlocking framework within a specific region.

At the same time, we need to be trans-regional in our thinking. Right now, what do we make of the fact that trans people are being denied their rights in places like Poland, Romania, and Hungary, and that gender is being taken out of the school curriculum in France? And how *does* this relate to what's happening in the Middle

East, in Palestine? What are the links? What are the incommensurabilities? I sometimes think that if we are just regional in our analysis, we miss the trans-regional ties. We miss the larger question of how the family and its heteronormative framework is being solidified under conditions of militarization, but also through neoliberalism and within certain religious frameworks. What is the relationship between the heteronormative family and the state, and how do we have a trans-regional analysis of that?

Of course, we need regional specificity, but we also need the trans-regional ties. Not just to have a better trans-regional analysis, but also to find the sites of alliance and solidarity that exist there.

ILAN PAPPÉ: We cannot ignore the pandemic, so I will finish with a question on COVID-19 and its impact. In a recent talk, you analyzed the way both optimistic and pessimistic leftist notions generated by COVID-19 were somewhat misguided—these are my words. You powerfully commented that it seems the neoliberal world was very quick to impose its morality and codex on the new reality, by talking about the health of the economy rather than the health of the people. It particularly ignored the health of those in the neoliberal capitalist world who have already been the "collateral damage" of a "healthy" economy, even before the pandemic. The proportional number of fatalities in minority communities in the UK, US, and places such as Brazil attest to it.

In this respect, my worry is that very much as in the case of Occupy Wall Street and the Arab uprisings, the commitment to resist social, economic, and political injustices is an energetic reaction against the apparent neoliberal abuse of the pandemic—but one that yet again is not translated into a sustained social movement of change. Are we putting aside once more, as in 2008 and in the Arab world in 2012, the necessity to organize, coordinate, and create an international counter-alliance to the one that degrades human life and well-being, especially under the panic of the pandemic? Can the more traditional left still contribute in this respect, by offering unions and even parties? Or are you content with more anarchic and sporadic shows of anger and protest, which do change the media discourse and maybe have an impact on its agenda?

This is also true to the solidarity movement with Palestine. And in a way, it goes back to your first answer about international networking—whether it is against this kind of work that Chomsky now called "the biofeudalism" of the pharmaceutical giants who use the pandemic, or the old oppression of corporations.

JUDITH BUTLER: At the beginning of the pandemic, there were people like Arundhati Roy who talked about the pandemic as a possible portal unto a different future. And I think my colleague Angela Davis also thought bringing the economy to a halt might allow us to take a collective historical moment to reflect on what the economy ought to look like, let's not rebuild in the same way. Of course, I also have that hope—there's no way *not* to have that hope. At the same time, from the very beginning there were those who said, "This is going to bolster the power of pharmaceuticals. This is going to bolster state monitoring and surveillance powers more generally." And that the pandemic will exacerbate geopolitical inequalities and racial inequality within local, regional, and global spheres.

We have, no doubt, seen the intensification of radical inequality. We see that through the ways in which the vaccine has been distributed, the ways in which vaccines are affordable, and which countries have them and are rapidly vaccinating everyone, and which do not. Israel has unjustly received praise for vaccinating those who live within '48, but even within '48 I'd like to know how many of those are Jewish and how many of those are not Jewish. The lack of access to vaccines within Palestine is abominable and not properly covered by the media, including the left media. So, we do see the intensification of racial and social class inequalities—there's no question about it.

But the fact that we see them, that they're brought into relief, can also be a cause for some optimism because it's rather hard to deny. Those inequalities are made much more explicit and so become available to a certain kind of tracking—historically, politically, culturally. I don't think that the pessimists or the optimists are "misguided." There is no way not to feel *both*. In other words, I feel both. I think many people oscillate between optimism and pessimism.

Climate change has received a new attention, in part because we understand the interconnected world a bit better by virtue of the pandemic. The pandemic is a disease of the interconnected world. So, once we understand the interconnected world, what does that say about labor? What does it say about resources? What does it say about global inequalities, corporate power and its effect? What does it say about decolonial structures? It gives us another framework outside of nationalism and individualism. And I can only hope that both of those ideologies are more firmly displaced in the course of our thinking and reacting to the pandemic.

Noam Chomsky

ON IMPASSE, INTERNATIONALISM, AND RADICAL CHANGE

April 22, 2021

N oam Chomsky, Laureate Professor of Linguistics at the University of Arizona, is widely regarded as the world's foremost public intellectual. First known for his pathbreaking linguistic work, Chomsky came to political prominence on account of his outspoken opposition to the US invasion of Vietnam. An icon of the New Left, he has since established an international reputation as a socialist activist and critic of US foreign policy, neoliberal state capitalism, the American news media, and the Israeli colonization of Palestine. As part of his voluminous scholarly output, Chomsky's research on the Palestine question dissects the historical and contemporary role of the United States in underwriting and facilitating Israel's systematic dispossession of the Palestinians. His best-selling works include *Syntactic Structures* (1957); *Peace in the Middle East? Reflections on Justice and Nationhood* (1974); *The Fateful Triangle: The United*

States, Israel, and the Palestinians (1983); *Manufacturing Consent: The Political Economy of the Mass Media* (1988); and *Understanding Power* (2002). He recently published his collected interviews by C.J. Polychroniou, including *Illegitimate Authority: Facing the Challenges of Our Time* (2023) and *A Livable Future Is Possible: Confronting the Threats to Our Survival* (2024), both with Haymarket Books.

ILAN PAPPÉ: Noam, it is wonderful to see you and to talk to you again. Thank you for taking the time. In 1967, you wrote an article on the responsibility of the intellectual, a piece that influenced my life. Not immediately—I was thirteen years old when the article appeared, so it happened a bit later! In 2019, an event organized to discuss this article at University College London (UCL) was censored, showing that your work is still regarded as dangerous and subversive to the powers that be.

This continued censorship of your article more than fifty years later raises the question whether much has changed. Does the new generation of intellectuals, of scholars, maturing into the twenty-first century still share in that responsibility? I ask you to look beyond Britain to the USA to say whether anything has changed in that part of the world, given your bleak view on American complicity in criminal policies at the time. This dates back to Southeast Asia in the early 1960s up to American involvement in the continued oppression of the Palestinians today. Has anything changed in Americans' sense of responsibility, or even in the readiness to assume accountability for what is done overseas in their name, quite often with their intellectual support and money? Are we in a better position today when it comes to the courage and commitment of intellectuals?

NOAM CHOMSKY: Let me start by making a comment, something few people know about the article you refer to. It first appeared in

1966, in a place that would surprise you: the journal of the Hillel Foundation at Harvard University. That's a very significant fact. In 1966, I gave a talk to the Hillel Foundation and they published it in their journal, *Mosaic*. In 1966, it was still possible to talk about Israel, Palestine, and the United States. From 1967, it became virtually impossible. Anyone who tried to mention it was a pariah.

A few years later in 1972, Abba Eban, the Israeli foreign minister at the time, had an article in the liberal Zionist magazine, *The Congress Weekly*, which was published by the American Jewish Congress. His article informed American Jews of their responsibility: to show that there is no difference between anti-Zionism and antisemitism. And anti-Zionism meant criticism of his government, the Labor government in Israel.

Eban gave two examples of how dangerous this anti-Zionism was. He was talking about what he called "Jewish self-hatred" and he named two people. I was one. Izzy Stone, I. F. Stone, was the other—a dedicated Zionist, but critical of Israeli government policies.

Eban says on the one hand, there are non-Jews who are antisemites. On the other hand, there are Jews who are consumed with a neurotic Jewish self-hatred. So that covers the spectrum. According to Eban, anyone critical of the government of Israel is an antisemite—and "it's your duty to show it, Jewish community." You have recently heard the same message in England very prominently. The way of destroying Jeremy Corbyn and a progressive Labour Party, by showing that anyone critical of Israel is an antisemite. They don't put it in those words, but that's what it amounts to.

Well, how much have things changed? Somewhat. For example, a kind of a bellwether of American intellectual opinion is the *New York Review of Books*, the major journal of left-liberal American intellectuals. Up until maybe two or three years ago, this regime held. It was impossible to discuss the issue. I used to write for the

New York Review regularly, but not after I became publicly involved in Israel-Palestine issues. After that, anathema.

It has changed in the last year or two, strikingly. If you read the journal now, you can read highly critical articles of Israeli policy, typically by Israeli writers. That makes the criticism sort of tolerable. There's a very strong article by Nathan Thrall that appeared in a recent issue. All of this reflects changes in public opinion in the United States. Those changes ultimately reflect themselves in intellectual opinion and maybe someday in policy. That's a matter of some significance.

But as Israeli policies became more and more brutal, reactionary, and intolerable, general liberal opinion has shifted. People who identify themselves as liberal Democrats have shifted away from the almost Stalinist-style support for Israel to more support for Palestinian rights. And it's showing up in the intellectual journals and it may show up in policy. Israel used to be the liberal darling in the United States, you couldn't say a word about it. It wasn't just not being able to write—meetings were broken up. I had to have police protection if I tried to talk about the topic, even in my own university. That's all changed.

Now, it is quite possible in these circles to be very critical of Israel. Support for Israel has shifted to the evangelical community, which is huge in the United States, and to ultraright nationalists, military and security, and the "committed." That also leaves opportunities for change in policies—we haven't seen it yet, but this has a way of affecting things. So with regard to intellectuals, yes, there has been a change, largely caused by Israel's violence and brutality.

I give talks on this constantly, and you could see exactly when it turned. [Operation] Cast Lead, for example—the 2006 Israeli invasion of Lebanon—had a big effect. Before that I was still getting police protection, but after I was drawing big crowds. I was giving the same talks. The more Israel moves to the right—the more brutal and harsh its policies become, the harder they are to suppress—the more we see changes in attitudes. Also among intellectuals, and, to a limited extent, in the press.

That's the way things change, that's how activism on the ground has a way of shifting attitudes. It means shifting what is sometimes called the Overton window—the range of things we are permitted to talk about within the mainstream framework. You can push a little at the edges and if the proper activities are undertaken, it could have an effect on policy.

ILAN PAPPÉ: In many ways I would share your optimism, although in the United Kingdom, and also in Palestine, there are countermeasures taken from above—by individual people and local lobbies. In the UK the Prevent program also targets any events that deal with criticism of Israel. Recently, we've been exposed to a different kind of assault on freedom of speech when it comes to Israel and Palestine through the new definitions of the Holocaust denial, where criticism of Israel is equated with antisemitism and denial of the Holocaust. Just recently, the secretary of state for higher education, Gavin Williamson, considered withdrawing funding for universities if they do not endorse the International Holocaust Remembrance Alliance (IHRA) definition of Holocaust denial. This is a definition that equates criticism of Israel with Holocaust denial, as I mentioned before.

We had a debate about the IHRA issue at the Institute recently, and our students raised concerns that echoed how you felt at the time about the Boycott, Divestment, Sanctions (BDS) movement. You raised this concern in our joint book, *On Palestine*, among other places. On the one hand, there is a wish to continue struggling in this country—and also I suppose in the United States—against any attempt to silence criticism of Israel by weaponizing antisemitism as a principal tool of intimidation. On the other hand, there is a worry that freedom of speech, rather than the plight of the Palestinians, becomes the main focus of the solidarity movement. How can we balance both legitimate concerns, without forgetting the primary motivation for solidarity? Because many people feel that one comes at the expense of the other. I know that this is one of the worries you had at the time, where a focus on freedom of speech rather than the topic that freedom of speech is supposed to serve, would divert attention from the real issues at hand.

NOAM CHOMSKY: I think the increase in intensity of efforts to silence discussion on this topic is a sign of increased desperation among supporters of Israeli policy. As they see the control of opinion slipping out of their hands, they're resorting to harsher and more desperate measures to try to block any discussion, any condemnation. In a way, it's sort of a good sign to see the extremism of attempts to silence discussion—it means the situation is getting out of their control.

It used to be much easier in England. In the late '80s or '90s, the editor of *Index on Censorship*, which is concerned with issues of freedom of expression, decided that it would be interesting to try to open the discussion to an area that George Orwell wrote about: suppression of thought in free societies. The journal had been focused on Eastern Europe and attempts to silence dissidents there—the editor himself was an Eastern European dissident. I should mention that Orwell's essay about how unpopular ideas can be suppressed without the use of force in "free" England was itself suppressed. His introduction to *Animal Farm* was published only thirty years later.

The editor of *Index* wanted to do the same thing: open up *Index on Censorship* for just one article about how ideas are suppressed within free societies. So I wrote an article on how discussion of Israel/Palestine is suppressed in the United States without the use of force, by other means. The roof fell in—he had to retire and the journal was closed. There was a huge attack on *Index* for allowing this to happen. It turned out later that the attack was initiated and orchestrated by a leading exponent of freedom of speech and a person who was an old friend, Isaiah Berlin.

The journal was later reconstituted and it hasn't gone in this dangerous direction again in the years that followed. That was then—you could just silence things. Now, it's not so easy. It's harder and therefore the effort to follow Abba Eban's advice from fifty years ago, to tar any criticism of Israel with antisemitism, has intensified. I think it's all reflection of the fact that, indeed, Israeli policies are becoming increasingly difficult to defend. And it's necessary for them to resort to means of suppressing opinion—if possible, shifting the topic to antisemitism in order to marginalize criticism.

However, segments of the left, very mistakenly, are joining this—not on the issue of criticizing Israel, but on other things. What's called "cancel culture" is an effort to try to prevent the kind of talk that they don't want to hear. It's wrong in principle and it's a gift to the right wing. What it means is those who have power will use it for their interests. So, yes, these problems arise all the time, and you need to keep your eyes on the main issue. The main problem is not academic freedom in Britain and the United States—it's the plight of the Palestinians. Anything that diverts attention from that, from what's going on and what we can do about it, is completely wrong.

And there is a lot that can be done, including things that are not discussed, possibly because they're so important. When something very topical is not discussed, you should be concerned. For example, there is something that, on the surface, doesn't appear to be related to Israel/Palestine, but in fact is very closely related. That's Iran. Right now it's on front pages, there is constant talk of the "great threat of Iranian nuclear weapons programs"—supposed programs. There's a sense that we need to do something about it.

Actually, there's something very simple to do, which everyone knows but no one is allowed to talk about. That has to do with Israel. A very simple way to solve the alleged problem of Iranian nuclear weapons is to institute a nuclear weapons–free zone in the Middle East. That would reduce tensions and have enormous positive effects. Why isn't it being done? Iran is strongly in favor of it and the Arab states have been strongly in favor of it for thirty years. The Global South is overwhelmingly in support of it. There is no criticism from Europe—they would go along with it. The option is blocked because the United States vetoes it, most recently under Obama. And the United States vetoes it because it does not want Israeli nuclear weapons to be open to inspection. In fact, the United States does not acknowledge the existence of nuclear weapons in Israel, though it's not in doubt. And the reason is that American law would come into play, raising the question of whether any US aid to Israel is legal.

It is an important point that could be pushed by an activist group. They could bring to the American public the fact that we're facing serious threats of war in order to preserve the huge flow of military and economic aid to Israel, and to Egypt, incidentally. These points have a lot of resonance among the American population, and they could lead to raising serious questions about the nature of US support for Israel. Even a hint of withdrawing support would have a big impact on Israel's policies. Israel has been very dependent on the United States for support since the 1970s, when Israel adopted a clear policy of choosing expansion over security. This meant relying on the United States for protection—it is a very fragile system.

These are possible actions that could be done immediately with a big effect on global politics, and in particular on Israel/Palestine. But they're not presented to you every day in the newspapers—you need to think them through and see the interconnections. And there are many.

ILAN PAPPÉ: Yes, I am as optimistic as you are about changes in the media, even when reading the more respectable American and British media outlets. Being a fellow in an Institute of Arab and Islamic Studies, with colleagues who are experts on the history and present realities in the Arab and Muslim worlds, there still is a sense that even the best of the media provides a very superficial, sometimes even malicious, framing of the Arab world. For instance, the idea that sectarianism has been in the Arab world since time immemorial, which gives little hope for reasonable, rational solutions. Or that religion in the Middle East always is fanatical. Those of us who study history and present realities in the region always worry about how distorted and destructive these images are.

With this in mind, I would like to move away from Palestine and ask how you see the impact of social movements in the United States. For the time being, the Black Lives Matter movement appears to be successful, while the jury is out on social movements like Occupy Wall Street. How do you view the future of these social movements? If I may add to this, how do you view the special circumstances in which we live now due to the COVID-19 pandemic? Some people optimistically believe that the pandemic inadvertently opened new vistas and opportunities for creating a counter-alliance of internationalism and solidarity that challenges the neoliberal capitalist interpretation and praxis of internationalism. Based on narrow economic interest and projects of privatization, a neoliberal vision of internationalism perpetuates the social and economic marginalization of nonwhite and nonelite groups.

Is there a new hope for counter-internationalism coming out of the pandemic? Can it take place only in the virtual world? How far can—and should—it take place on the ground, as before the age of internet? And are you hopeful that these mass movements can still have an impact on policies from above, whether American domestic and foreign policy, or other countries' foreign policies?

NOAM CHOMSKY: Let's look at those movements that you mentioned. The best way to think about those kinds of questions is very concretely. What has been done? What can be done? Let's take the Occupy movement, which is widely believed to have failed. I was very much involved in it and I don't think it failed—I think it was a big success. Remember that Occupy was not a strategy, it was a short-term tactic. You can't occupy Zuccotti Park forever, only for a couple of months.

During its brief period, the Occupy tactic broke open the issue of radical inequality, which had been suppressed. It became a major issue, which other movements and policy focused on. That's a breakthrough, it's an achievement. But more was hoped for—activists in Occupy were hoping to carry out neighborhood organizing on similar issues. They succeeded to some extent, but not as much as what was hoped. That's the way movements work.

Now let's look at Black Lives Matter. The movement has been enormously successful, even before the murder of George Floyd. Black Lives Matter had penetrated large parts of American society, not only the Black community, and had general popularity way beyond what social movements ordinarily have. After the Floyd assassination, it just exploded. There were massive demonstrations all over—solidarity, Blacks and whites together. These were overwhelmingly peaceful demonstrations, with maybe a little bit of property destruction around the fringes. But of course that was what the right-wing media focused on.

Black Lives Matter had two-thirds popular support in the United States—that is incredible for a popular movement. It's far beyond what Martin Luther King had, even at the peak of his popularity, and it remains very high. Of course, the right wing is making extreme efforts to try to demonize the movement, saying it was all about violence, trying to murder whites, and so on and so forth. Just about every Republican state right now is either considering or passing legislation to effectively ban popular demonstrations.

For example, the state of Oklahoma just made it legitimate for the driver of a car to hit, and even kill, demonstrators, under some false pretense. These legislations show desperation across the board to try to stop popular activism. And there are parallel efforts in Republican states to prevent voting, specifically to reduce the danger of popular votes. That's desperation. And unfortunately, there is support for it—Trump was brilliant at tapping the poisons that run just beneath the surface of American society, giving them justification. It's leading to a very serious problem. Almost half the population is now consumed with terror about what's called "the great replacement"—that the white, traditionally Christian population is being overwhelmed and destroyed, faced with genocide by immigrants and Blacks.

I'm old enough to remember this in the 1930s—the reaction to the growth of successful popular movements, which are having a major impact. The [Bernie] Sanders campaign was an astonishing success that broke with over a century of American political history. American elections are pretty much bought by concentrations of economic power—you can predict the outcome of an election with remarkable probability, simply by looking at campaign spending. Sanders totally changed that. He became the most popular political figure in the country and virtually won nomination with no support from wealth or power. He faced the same kind of attacks that we saw against Corbyn in the British media, whether ignoring, denunciation, or lies. But he broke through. He is now the head of one of the most important committees in the Senate, the Budget Committee, with major influence. Others came in on the Sanders wave and the movements are increasing.

All of this can continue to happen. Now, what about the effect of the pandemic? Looking at it closely tells you a lot about our culture and our level of civilization. The question is international, like global warming and other major crises—there are no boundaries, which is obvious in the case of Covid.

It's very striking to see what is happening. It's understood by everyone that unless vaccines go quickly to the poor areas—to Africa, Asia, and other regions—the virus will mutate and lead to new variants. Some may be extremely lethal, like Ebola, and some may be uncontrollable. It will come back and hit the rich, it will devastate them. That's known.

So what are the rich countries doing about it? They are preventing vaccines from going to the poor areas. Rich countries are monopolizing vaccines, well beyond what they can use. They are storing vaccines "just in case," not distributing them to the poor countries, even though leadership knows very well that this is a suicidal course. If you are the leader of a rich country, it's more important to guarantee the profits of big pharmaceutical corporations, their "intellectual property rights," than to save yourself from destruction. Let alone the ethical issue of how many Africans and Asians will be killed. This tells you something about the level of civilization in the highest circles.

But actually there are a few countries who are internationalist—one in particular: Cuba. It's the one genuinely internationalist country in the world, which sends doctors all over. A year ago, at the beginning of the pandemic in Europe, there was a serious outbreak in northern Italy. Northern Italy happens to be very close to two rich countries, Germany and Austria, that are in the same union as Italy—the European Union. At that point, rich countries had the pandemic fairly under control, they had lots of resources. Did Germany and Austria send any help to northern Italy? No.

But Cuba was willing to send doctors to northern Italy during the pandemic. A couple of weeks ago, the US Department of Health and Human Services issued its 2020 report, the last under the Trump administration. It is full of self-congratulation. If you read it closely, there's an interesting paragraph buried inside, which details how the United States is reacting to the Covid epidemic in places of severe outbreak, like South America or in Panama. The department congratulates themselves on having pressured the government of Panama to refuse and remove the Cuban doctors who had come to assist—because "we have to stop Cuba's malign influence in the western hemisphere."

In the headlines you read that Brazil is a disaster area, they don't have vaccines. Yet the United States praises themselves for having convinced the government of Brazil not to accept the offer of vaccines from Russia, which are exactly the same as Western vaccines. And that's happening worldwide. There is pressure to develop a "people's vaccine," which will break the monopolies—much of the pressure comes from countries like Cuba and China, who claim that they will provide free vaccines. Whether or not they will, I don't know. But the rich and powerful are refusing. The United States has an excess of vaccines that it cannot use, which is all piling up in warehouses.

President Biden graciously decided to release some of the vaccine excess to other countries. Which ones? Canada, which is the world champion in storing vaccines that it cannot use. What about Asia or Africa? Mexico is the second country that received vaccines from the US, as part of a bribe to the Mexican government to prevent desperate refugees from fleeing to the American border. That's called "generosity," in terms of Western civilization, and it is beyond what the European countries are doing.

So, what are the prospects for internationalism? I don't see it from leadership. Maybe there can be popular movements on the ground, moving toward genuine internationalism on all fronts. Saving ourselves from destruction by the next pandemic and overcoming the desperate crisis of environmental destruction can be done. But it's not going to come from leadership. It can come from popular activist pressures, the way things have happened in the past. That's what we need to look at.

ILAN PAPPÉ: My last question actually ties in with your final remark about where we should hope for change—not coming from the elite, but rather from social movements who share international solidarity. International agendas can eventually influence local struggles, like the movement for freedom and liberation in Palestine. And this really is a question for our student community—those who work on decolonization, those who work in Palestine, or those who work in other parts of the world. Many ask themselves about the utility of believing that one can change politics from above or from within, in their own personal careers. Or should they hope, maybe even cherish the prospect of being part of grassroots movements of revolution—involved in radical action from below and by that contribute to more just society?

For instance, can what you termed many years ago a "corporatocracy" be reformed from within? Or can it only be challenged from the outside? This is a question of a career pattern for our graduates, whose healthy instincts against injustice will hopefully stay with them for as long as possible.

NOAM CHOMSKY: Well, the official line, which one should always view with considerable skepticism, is that "changes come from leadership." Enlightened leadership views the situation realistically, the intelligent men of the community—men, of course—think things through and decide what is right, and then they make decisions to the benefit of all. That's what you learn in school, that's what you read in the newspapers.

There's an element of truth to it. When legislation is passed, it's passed in Congress or Parliament. When decisions are made in corporate boardrooms, they're made in corporate boardrooms. But why are they made? Why some decisions and not others? Here we go back to the popular forces that are changing the conditions under which decisions are made. If you leave it to corporate boardrooms, they'll use fossil fuels to the maximum. "It doesn't matter if fossil fuels destroy the world—who cares? We'll make more profit tomorrow." It's the nature of the institution.

Go to the top banks. They'll invest in fossil fuels because they can make money that way. They know the consequences, but this doesn't fit within the institutional framework. The same is true of legislatures. On the other hand, if corporate boardrooms look out the window and see what they describe as "the peasants coming with the pitchforks"—reputational risk, in polite terms—then groups of leading CEOs and major business groups will address the public. They will say, "Yes, we realize that we've made mistakes, but now we are going to overcome them." They claim to become what used to be called "soulful corporations," "who will work for the benefit of the common good, so trust us and go home."

And they will actually do something, which is not meaningless. You can press them to do things that are worth doing, like getting the banks to reduce their investment in fossil fuels. On the other hand, if you look closely when ExxonMobil says, "OK, we realize that we did something wrong, we need to work on renewable energy," they're putting money into sustainable energy through carbon capture. That is, technologies that will allow them to continue to use fossil fuels to the maximum. Because maybe, somehow, someone will figure out a way to get the poison out of the air after we put it in. Those are the things we need to be looking for.

It's the same in the political system. Some people in the political system genuinely want significant change—in the United States, we just saw it two days ago. Alexandria Ocasio-Cortez, one of the young representatives who came in on the Sanders wave, and Ed Markey, a senator from Massachusetts who has been interested in the environment his entire career, instituted legislation on a Green New Deal. This is exactly what needs to be done. It is detailed and feasible—worked out as to how it will provide a better life, better jobs, and overcome the climate crisis. The deal is now on the legislative agenda. And that is a result of a great deal of activism on the part of mostly young people, like Extinction Rebellion and the Sunrise Movement. That's how things change.

So, yes, decisions are made in the Senate, in Parliament, in the corporate boardrooms—but under circumstances and conditions that are established, to a significant extent, by popular action, activism, and demands. That interaction is there. It has always been and it will continue to be. It's not one or the other, but both.

Angela Y. Davis

TOWARD TRANSNATIONAL
MOVEMENTS FOR JUSTICE

January 28, 2021

Angela Y. Davis, Distinguished Professor Emerita of History of Consciousness and Feminist Studies, UCSC, is known internationally for her ongoing work to combat all forms of oppression in the United States and abroad. Over the years she has been active as a student, teacher, writer, scholar, and activist/organizer. She is a living witness to the historical struggles of the contemporary era. Davis emerged as a leading activist in the 1960s in the Communist Party USA and had close relations with the Black Panther Party. During the past fifty years, she has continued to be at the cutting edge of radical thought, prison abolition, and movement organizing. She is a founding member of Critical Resistance,[1] a national organization dedicated to the dismantling of the prison industrial complex as the system that links government with industry and drives the proliferation of prisons and prisoners.[2] Internationally, she is affiliated with Sisters Inside, an abolitionist organization based in Queensland, Australia, that works in solidarity with women in prison. Her works include *Women, Race and Class* (1981), *Are Prisons Obsolete?* (2003), *The Meaning of Freedom: And Other Difficult Dialogues* (2012), *Freedom Is a Constant Struggle: Ferguson, Palestine, and the Foundations of a Movement* (2016), and *Abolition. Feminism. Now.*, with Gina Dent, Erica R. Meiners, and Beth E. Richie (2022).

ILAN PAPPÉ: Angela, it is a great pleasure and honor to have you with us. Your stance, career, and courage are a model for how to fuse activism with scholarship, and moral commitment with professionalism—without fear and without caving to intimidation and persecution. We confront this pressure sometimes at the European Centre for Palestine Studies due to our principles, values, and moral stances, and I know that you face it regularly as a scholar and activist. Everyone would love us to begin our conversation with your thoughts about what happened in the United States on Capitol Hill on the 6th of January 2021. What is your assessment of this event and how do you contextualize it in America today? What does it mean for the future?

ANGELA Y. DAVIS: First of all, let me tell you, Ilan, what an honor it is to finally meet you after reading your work and following your career. To venture a response to your question, I would begin by saying that I was shocked, of course, by this display of organized white supremacist violence. But I cannot say that I was entirely surprised. I interpret this attempted insurrection instigated by the 45th president of the United States during the last days of his office as a desperate attempt to turn the tide of history. Not only to reverse the recent election results, but to reverse decades of struggle against racism that have yielded very important victories.

The insurrectionists and many Trump supporters around the country have been persuaded by the demagogy of the last four years that white people have necessarily suffered as a result of progress in the struggles for justice for Black, Latinx, Indigenous, and other people of color. In other words, they interpret what we see as the beginning of racial justice to be white oppression. They assume that communities of color can only move forward if white people are relegated to positions historically occupied by Black people and other people of color. But they fail to recognize that when Black people achieve progress, it almost always means better conditions for poor white people. They misread the increasing impoverishment of white people by failing to recognize the destructive impact of capitalism—global capitalism, racial capitalism. And in that context, we recently learned that the wealth of billionaires in this country has increased tremendously during the COVID-19 pandemic.

As we already know, their total wealth is two-thirds higher than the wealth held by the bottom half of the population. So I just want to say parenthetically that Naomi Klein's analysis of disaster capitalism helps us to understand what is happening here.[3] To conclude this answer, I would say that the insurrection on January 6th was a microcosmic representation of the failed efforts to turn back the clock. Not only with respect to challenges to racism, but also patriarchy, transphobia, climate justice, and the assaults on the working class. It seems to me that it represented a desperate effort to return to a time when racism, misogyny, environmental pollution, and all of this represented the uncontested foundation of our social realities.

ILAN PAPPÉ: It's very important that you mentioned the notion that this is a "zero-sum" game. If an oppressed group gains more privileges, or rights rather than privileges, and it is not perceived as a win-win situation. We see this also on the ground in Palestine, where most Israeli Jews think that any enhancement or improvement in Palestinian rights means that their own rights will be diminished. This is important for many of us.

As you say, white supremacism was at the heart of this attack on Capitol Hill. In the whirlwind of the two days that followed, many Palestinians who live in America noticed Nancy Pelosi's speech, which she opened by referring to an Israeli poet. In our struggle to make America a place where the Palestinian narrative is heard, where the case of Palestine is not ignored, we could not miss this. Pelosi started her speech by quoting Ehud Manor, who wrote a poem about his loyalty to the white Israeli settler colonialist state despite feeling uncertain about its actions. She then went on to mention her visit to Yad Vashem, the Holocaust museum in Israel.

If you listened to Pelosi, you would have thought that a group of antisemites and anti-Zionists had attacked Capitol Hill—this was the essence of it.

The appearance of the Israeli narrative and Israel's supporters in the Democratic Party is worrying. When President Obama was elected, one of the first venues he went to was to AIPAC (the American Israel Public Affairs Committee). Even in that dramatic moment in America's life, Israel and its supporters were there.

ANGELA Y. DAVIS: As you know, the political establishment in the United States, the Democratic Party as well as the Republican Party, is closely linked to Zionism. But let me begin by making another point. It is very important to identify connections between anti-Black racism and antisemitism. And it is important to remember the historical alliances that brought Black and Jewish communities together to speak out against the violence that was inflicted on both communities by groups such as the Ku Klux Klan and the

White Citizens' Councils. Growing up in the city of Birmingham, Alabama, which was the most segregated city in the US, I remember that when Black churches were bombed, Jewish synagogues were also bombed. I want to be clear about the importance of making that connection. But at the same time, I think that Nancy Pelosi is probably reluctant to acknowledge the fact that charges of antisemitism have been tied to critiques of the state of Israel in existing political discourse. These historical linkages of racism and antisemitism are not recognized in the way they should be.

Under the occupation of Palestine by the state of Israel, Palestinians suffer forms of oppression that are akin to the ways in which Black people have been treated in the US. I've been following the case of the killing of Ahmad Erekat, who is the cousin of my friend and comrade Noura Erakat. His killing is so reminiscent of the killing of Mike Brown in Ferguson, Missouri—he was killed as he was raising his hands. We all remember the slogan, "Hands up. Don't shoot."

It seems that these historical alliances and recognitions of the kinship between anti-Black racism, white supremacy, antisemitism need to be brought to the fore in a way that also highlights the Israeli occupation of Palestine, the dispossession of the Palestinian people, and the deep kinship of Zionism and racism. We really need to challenge the efforts to define antisemitism as a critique of the state of Israel.

ILAN PAPPÉ: Let me move ahead to another topic. You have devoted your life to the struggle for equality—not only for African Americans, but also women, workers, and marginalized and oppressed groups. And not only in the United States. One of your comments after the murder of George Floyd and widespread activity by the Movement for Black Lives really interested me. You said that you were encouraged by the reaction among the white community to this particular crime. And as we know, the reaction went all over the world.

Does this reaction signify a fundamental change in attitudes toward African Americans in the US? And if it is a change, how deep does it go? I was surprised at how that crime seemed to catch the attention of white people, not only in the United States. Is it a sign of encouragement, rather than a superficial reaction? Is it something more fundamental in your eyes?

ANGELA Y. DAVIS: Yes, I was really encouraged by the fact that in the aftermath of the lynching of George Floyd and the police killing of Breonna Taylor, more white people participated in antiracist demonstrations than ever before in the entire history of this country. That was very heartening. But we know that the majority of white people voted for the 45th occupant of the White House—and the majority of white women voted for him. So I was encouraged and at the same time deeply disappointed. But it seems to me that those mass mobilizations that took place after the police murders of George Floyd and Breonna Taylor represented a kind of collective coming to consciousness about structural racism that has been long overdue.

For too long racism has been regarded as an individual flaw, a defect that can be removed by learning how not to express racist attitudes or use racist language. And the focus has been on distinguishing oneself as *not a racist*. How many times have we heard the phrase, "I am not a racist"? How many times have we heard the phrase, "I don't see race"? Or I've had people tell me, "Well, I don't think of you as a Black person." These efforts to challenge racism have been so overdetermined by an individualist approach that is connected to neoliberal ideologies and capitalist approaches. It has been very difficult to create a public discourse about institutional and structural racism—about racism that is deeply embedded in the structures of policing, incarceration, health care, education, and housing. So, my analysis of what happened in May is that the collective witnessing of the murder of George Floyd amounted to something similar to the audience of a lynching.

Because we all saw that video. We saw the last eight minutes of his life. And we were all aware that everyone else was watching. In the historical lynching parties, white people were supposed to be amused by watching the slow death of a Black person, which happened over and over in the aftermath of Reconstruction Era in the latter 1800s and early 1900s. And it seems to me that that moment when we were watching the death of George Floyd and aware of the fact that we were part of a large collective witnessing, it allowed for the emergence of a new consciousness—and not automatically or spontaneously, because this consciousness has been cultivated by young activists associated with the Black Lives Matter movement. We can go back to the movements that began in response to the killing of Trayvon Martin and the failure to hold other vigilante murderers accountable.

It is important to point out that activists and academics have been using the notion of structural racism for many decades, but it was superseded in popular discourse by the concept of racism as simply a trait of the individual. This is why people could argue that we were entering into a "post-racial era" when Obama was elected to the office of the presidency. I think it's also important to remember that we were at the beginning of the pandemic then, and the most striking example of structural racism was the fact that disproportionate numbers of Indigenous, Black, and Latinx people were being infected and dying from COVID-19. Those police killings helped to consolidate a popular awareness of structural racism and its impact on policing. And therefore I remain optimistic that it is possible to build on that collective recognition and begin to develop strategies that specifically target structural racism in all of these institutions.

ILAN PAPPÉ: The prison system is a particularly heinous and callous side of institutional racism in the United States that attracted your attention, especially the crimes of sterilization and incarceration. You are a great advocate for both defunding the police and abolition, which are the most difficult challenges for anyone facing institutional racism. This also resonates with many people in Britain who feel that the prison system is probably the most hidden and yet the most brutal side of institutional racism, even if racism is more visible in the police force or in their daily encounters with authority.

I wonder whether you feel any hope for the Biden administration regarding these particularly ugly and cruel manifestations of institutional racism as they appear in the prison system. Even without being experts, many of us outside the United States are familiar with and horrified by the prison system, including its neoliberal aspects. The privatization of the US prison system adds a sinister aspect to an already brutal system. Do you have any hope for the Biden administration? Or any hope at all without the Biden administration?

ANGELA Y. DAVIS: First of all, I am glad that at least for the moment, we were able to use the electoral system to defeat the onslaught of fascism. At the same time, Biden's past positions don't necessarily give me hope, nor do [Kamala] Harris's positions. But I do believe that they are more susceptible to the kind of pressure emanating from organized movements than the previous president. So I do have hope—but I don't simply have hope in the Biden administration. I have hope in the fact that that there are so many young people who ally themselves with politically radical and progressive positions. My hope is that we will continue to put pressure on those in office. Of course, we need to remember that Biden was one of the main architects of the 1994 Crime Bill, which is in part responsible for the emergence of what we call "mass incarceration."

It was good to see that the day before yesterday Biden issued an executive order which ends contracts with private prison companies. But it is important to point out that we challenge and stand up against the privatization of prisons not because we think that a prison system that is not privatized will work—but rather the privatization of prisons represents the role that capitalism has played in the development of a racist-inspired mass incarceration system. Federal prisons make up a pretty small fraction of the US prison system. And private prison companies run about twelve federal prisons that house about nine percent of all federal prisoners.[4] Simply ending contracts with private prison companies is not going to bring major transformations. An overwhelming majority of the more than two million people who are incarcerated in the US are in state, county, and local prisons or jails, and jails and prisons in Indian Country. They are also in immigrant detention facilities.

Private prisons house about eight percent of all incarcerated people. That is important, especially for those of us who are trying to point out the economic dimension of mass incarceration and the way in which it is linked to global capitalism and the deindustrialization processes that took people's jobs, access to housing and health care, and the dismantling of the welfare state. All of that is so important to understanding the pivotal role that capitalism has played in the production of such a huge carceral system. But simply targeting private prisons will not fundamentally change anything else. Because we actually see privatization within state-owned and -run facilities—the privatization of health care, goods and services, companies that provide meals, and the companies that provide the appliances that prisoners order.

So simply ending contracts with private prisons does not in any way begin to disrupt the relationship of prisons, the carceral system, to the system of global capitalism. There hasn't been structural change. And I think that the structural change can come. It can come from an insistence on abolition that is made by organized groups of people who are resisting. Let me tell you, Ilan, that I've been writing about abolition, along with many other people, since the 1970s. In 1971, the prisoners staged an uprising at Attica—a radical uprising in which they called for abolition. And since then, we developed a very strong abolitionist movement. Particularly a movement that recognizes the importance of gender and the connections with movements to challenge sexual violence.

But I never imagined that abolitionist discourse would enter the mainstream in my lifetime. I remember the way we talked about abolition as if it were so far in the future that we would never witness this kind of moment where there is serious engagement with the question of creating new modes of addressing health, safety, and security—that's what the movement to defund the police and abolish prisons is all about. It's about imagining and developing new institutions that can better address the question of safety and security in our society.

ILAN PAPPÉ: Speaking of hope and capitalism and its impact, perhaps it is a good moment to talk a little bit about the left. We have something in common in our biographies: we both were members of the Communist Party. Despite the differences between the United States and historical Palestine, one common feature troubles people who are on the left—and not just in the United States or Palestine. And this is all about the relationship between the wish to push forward a wholesale social revolution, with the stress on class consciousness and determination on the one hand, and the focus on identity politics on the other. The realization that a wider coalition is needed for the making of a more just, egalitarian society. This is a politics of identification.

In Palestine, and in particular in Israel, it is a search to connect not only the Palestinian victims of Zionism but also the Jewish ones (for instance the Ethiopian Jews and North African Jews) and the working class with the overall struggle for a democratic state that would be part of the Arab world and not a bastion of the West. But it has not worked very well because nationalism, religious fanaticism, and politics of identity stand in the way.

You have always struggled for a politics of identification in the USA. Right now, we see how neoliberal capitalist regimes have utterly failed to deal with the COVID-19 pandemic—the whole system is unable to cope without some sort of social welfare policy and nationalization. They cannot even begin to deal with both the economic crisis and the health crisis. This is a moment when the left must go back to its basic challenges and ask, "This time, can we have a stronger agenda that connects the different struggles locally, but also internationally?" And I hope that like me, you feel there are indications that this is possible. The question is, will we be able to exhaust this opportunity that history has given us? What are the chances of enhancing or even achieving this in the future?

ANGELA Y. DAVIS: First, many activists in the Black Lives Matter movement, and in other movements that focus specifically on racial justice, recognize that racial justice is inconceivable without the prospect of economic transformation and an end to capitalism. I still believe that revolutionary transformation absolutely requires a thoroughgoing challenge to capitalism. And some of us have never seen the struggle against racism separately from the struggle against capitalism. There are those who simply assume that bringing Black people higher up on the economic ladder—that is to say incorporating, diversifying the capitalist leadership—will bring about an end to racism. But regardless of who is at the helm of these efforts, whether it's white people or people of color, the structure remains the same. And I think that it's important to recognize that class consciousness is always linked to race and gender. I really like Stuart Hall's formulation: "Race is the modality in which class is lived." And I am also heartened by the fact that increasing numbers of people are beginning to use the term that was introduced by Cedric Robinson. That is to say "racial capitalism"—that capitalism has always been in relation to racism. That colonialism and slavery are at the very foundations of the development of capitalism, the primitive accumulation about which Marx writes. And so the challenge is to keep these things in tension, to recognize that they are not separate struggles. For too long, the left has assumed that the struggle to end capitalism is a white working-class struggle.

The working class has been largely defined as white in Europe and in the US. And struggles against racism have been assumed to only occupy the terrain of civil rights. Now we're recognizing that not only must the struggle against racism be central to challenges to capitalism, but challenges to racism cannot really move in a radical direction without also challenging capitalism. So I'm thinking about the trajectory of movements over the last period, during the first decades of the twenty-first century—let's not forget that it was the Occupy movement that began to demonstrate that it was possible to develop large, massive movements that were not necessarily organized in the way they were before.

It is essential to realize that the major struggles for democracy that have been effective, at least in this part of the world, have been initiated by Black people and people of color. To simply relegate these struggles to identity politics is not helpful. Everyone benefits when Black people make demands that allow us to move forward—not only other people of color and not only white progressive people, but the white people who assume that in order for their lives to matter, Black lives have to be snuffed out. I think that we're in the process of reconsolidating a left movement. The left does not look like it used to—it has very new faces.

It has been essential for us here in the US who are involved in these struggles to be able to learn from the Palestinian struggles. I can't emphasize enough that this current moment in our movement against racism has been in many ways assisted by Palestinian activists. I'm referring to the fact that in 2014, when the Ferguson protest happened, it was Palestinians and Palestine who provided the first example of international solidarity with Black movements unfolding here. As such, Palestinians were in the leadership of a global movement of solidarity.

And we've also learned so much about the importance of broadening our notion of carcerality—you've pointed out that Palestine is the largest prison in the world. How do we engage in struggles for abolition in this country while recognizing that oftentimes methods that are used to decarcerate actually spread carcerality in the community along trajectories that are very dangerous? We have a great deal of gratitude to our Palestinian comrades, sisters, and brothers for their work in Palestine, but also for assisting us to become more radical in our understanding of what it is we are doing.

ILAN PAPPÉ: Absolutely. I was deeply moved watching how during the attack on Gaza, people demonstrated in solidarity with Ferguson. It was amazing. We are nearing the end of our conversation, but I want to pose one last question about academic scholarship and activism. We have many young graduate students and undergraduate students with us, especially those who work on issues such as

Palestine, Black history, or decolonization. They are fusing scholarship with activism, and quite often they encounter criticism, prejudice, and hostile attitudes—all under the guise that what they're doing is not professional enough, that it is biased or not objective.

You and I have both faced our share of such criticism over the years. Like you, I have great faith in the younger generation. But we need to articulate the message for the next generation that academia is not a separate space in the moral struggle for a just society. And this is not easy. From your experience, and may I say also from mine, there is a personal price one might pay for being an outspoken person in academia on moral issues that counter mainstream attitudes, policies, and prejudices. We know the intimidation, the rules of the game. How can we ensure that the next generation does not relent in the face of this pressure? Do you see hope for moral activism within the scholarly community, or the continuation of "organic intellectuals," as Antonio Gramsci would put it?

ANGELA Y. DAVIS: I would begin by saying that even as we are critical of existing structures of education, including higher education, education matters. Knowledge matters. We cannot engage in successful efforts for radical transformation without knowledge. But at the same time, it's important for university-trained academics to recognize that knowledge is produced in many sites—not only the university. In this current moment in the US, when we are engaged in serious conversations about defunding the police and abolishing prisons, many of the ideas were first formulated by people who were incarcerated at the time they began to reflect on abolitionist principles.

Over the last few years I've been involved in the creation of "critical prison studies," an interdisciplinary field that has been embraced by increasing numbers of young scholars. And they recognize that the foundational knowledge of that field comes from people in prison themselves. I think it is important to demystify the process of producing knowledge, and at the same time recognize that scholar-activists need the training and exposure to ideas that the university can offer. But it also means that one must learn how to take advantage of these institutions of education and simultaneously be critical of them. The university is not unlike other terrains of struggle; we have to hold in tension our critiques of the institution and the training and knowledge practices that are offered to us.

I'm very excited because I think that this generation of young scholars is more equipped to engage in addressing the problems of the globe—for example, environmental justice and, of course, racism and heteropatriarchy. I've taught for many, many years in a feminist studies department and there's still a great deal of tension, particularly within academic feminism. But we've seen the emergence of theories and practices of feminism that disassociate themselves from the old notion that in order to be free, women simply have to try to rise up the ladder and puncture the glass ceiling. We see a feminism that is antiracist, that is anticapitalist, that explores intersectionalities. This is the feminism we need now. It's not always the feminism one sees at the university, but one witnesses the struggles and the tensions and the contradictions—and that is the context within which we always work.

Nadine El-Enany

ON COLONIAL VIOLENCE
AND ANTICOLONIAL RESISTANCE

May 27, 2021

N adine El-Enany is a writer, poet, and teacher. She is Professor of Law at the University of Kent. Her book *(B)ordering Britain: Law, Race and Empire* (Manchester University Press, 2020) rethinks what Britain is, arguing it is an imperial and colonial space produced through violent and extractive economies of empire and maintained through immigration law. This reframing troubles racial capitalist structures, challenges mythological narratives about Britain's colonial history, rejects a liberal politics of recognition, develops a methodology for anticolonial research in law, and paves the way for an empowering and radical politics of racial justice and migrant solidarity. *(B)ordering Britain* was awarded the 2021 Socio-Legal Theory and History Book Prize. El-Enany is coauthor of *Empire's Endgame: Racism and the British State* (Pluto Press, 2021) and coeditor of *After Grenfell: Violence, Resistance and Response* (Pluto Press,

2019). She is winner of a 2020 Philip Leverhulme Prize. She has written for the *Guardian*, *LRB* blog, *Verso* blog, *New Humanist*, *MAP Magazine*, *Open Democracy*, and *Critical Legal Thinking*. Her poetry has appeared in magazines including *Butcher's Dog*, *Magma*, *Propel Magazine*, *14 Magazine*, *fourteen poems*, *Gutter Magazine*, *Black Iris*, *Poetry Wales*, *Under the Radar*, *And Other Poems*, and the *Rialto*. She is winner of the Chancellor's Poetry Prize 2024, was shortlisted for the 2023 Poetry London Pamphlet Prize and longlisted for the 2023 and 2024 Rialto Nature and Place Poetry competitions and the 2022 Fish Poetry Prize.

ILAN PAPPÉ: Let us begin with a reference to the brutal Israeli attack on Gaza and other parts of historical Palestine,[1] seeing these events through the prism of your work and analysis. The recent assault highlighted the relevance of your work, also for the situation in Palestine.

I would like to offer two insights and hear your opinion. The first is the need for any solidarity movement to look first at the injustices in its own society, as a way of its solidarity with others. The second is the novel and crucial approach your work offers us to challenge the myths of Israel as a democratic state—a framing that is accepted by many people and immunizes Israel from condemnation for the brutality we have witnessed on the ground.

With the help of your book, *(B)ordering Britain: Law, Race and Empire*, let us look at how Israel and Britain are still, today, colonial spaces. And let us consider how solidarity in Britain, with the struggle of decolonization in historical Palestine, can be closely associated with decolonizing Britain.

Deconstructing what colonialism and decolonization means for the struggle for justice in Britain should be an integral part of the activism and solidarity movements against the settler-colonial project of Zionism and Israel in historical Palestine. So, my first question to you is: Do you see such a dialectical relationship? And does this account in some way for your clear support for the Palestinian liberation struggle?

NADINE EL-ENANY: I do see the dialectical relationship between the different anticolonial projects, including those in Britain and Palestine. But I want to start with what accounts for my clear support of the Palestinian struggle for freedom. Of course it is in part a result of my understanding of historical events and the structures and processes of colonization. The fact that they are ongoing in so many contexts helps me to frame and articulate the urgency of the struggle for Palestinian liberation.

But your question really made me think about it from a personal perspective. I know that I was a clear supporter of the Palestinian struggle from a very young age—certainly before the age when I would have had the level of understanding that I do now about colonialism, its structures, and the role of law in perpetuating colonial violence.

I think I had a clear support for Palestinian struggle from the age at which we all will become aware, if we take an interest in what is happening around us and in the news—when we begin to see and feel in some ways, viscerally and painfully, the pain of others and the injustice that people are experiencing. I felt this at an early age. The local pro-Palestinian rallies in Exeter, organized by the local Stop the War branch, were the first demonstrations I went on, including alone, as a teenager.

And ironically, it was this outrage, deep sadness, and empathy that actually drove me to set aside various other passions I had as a young person and choose to study law. Because I felt that law held this power to do something about injustice. That we could rely on law, that we could invoke law to do something in a humanitarian way. Naively, I thought that if I studied law this would help the situation.

Now, so much of my work is about critiquing the potential of law to radically change situations of oppression, which I'm sure we will speak about and I discuss in my book at length. I've spent a lot of time trying to bring histories of colonialism to bear on our understanding of contemporary violence and injustice.

I also want to say something about the myth of Israel as a democratic state. As you say, in my work I tried to dispel the myth that Britain is a postimperial, legitimately bordered, sovereign nation-state. Challenging this myth is the first step toward a project of practically dismantling the violent border regime. The myth that Israel is a democratic state has a similar kind of cataclysmic power in how we begin to understand, or not understand, particular situations. And I know your own efforts in busting these myths in your work around Israel in particular. It is important to dwell on the status and power of these kinds of myths because they are actually what obstruct the very kind of solidarity that Palestinians are calling for, and that we are calling for—the kind that supports the Palestinian struggle for liberation.

To my mind, then, the question is: What is this liberation from, precisely? We can only call for liberation of a people if first we recognize that people are oppressed. On hearing an allegation of oppression targeted at a state that is assumed to be democratic, progressive, or even world-leading on human rights, I can see how some people might struggle to make sense of this kind of accusation.

I suppose this is how myths work, because Israel cannot be a democratic state and be an apartheid state—it cannot be a democratic state and a settler-colonial power at the same time. Britain cannot be a domestic space of colonialism and also a postimperial, legitimately bordered, sovereign nation-state. Because there are certain principles that underlie a democratic state, like the rule of law and equality before the law.

These principles cannot be sustained in a context in which a section of the population is oppressed, regarded and treated as non-human, subject to targeted state violence and murder daily. Where state laws and policies are specifically designed to promote and propagate the supremacy of one section of the population. These laws and policies are also designed to cleanse the land of another section of the population through police and military violence, evictions, the destruction and occupation of property, allowing violent groups to torment people and act with impunity, controlling the economy to ensure a specific part cannot survive, thrive, or flourish. And through legal judgments, which replicate and legitimize that violence.

We can clearly see how powerful and harmful these kinds of myths are, how they distort reality. As you say, for more than ten days Israel has been carrying out airstrikes, dropping bombs in a densely populated area in which people—families—are under siege or trapped with nowhere to go. They are traumatizing and killing an already traumatized population. To my mind, it was as though people elsewhere seemed to notice this violence. Suddenly, in this so-called exchange of fire, children are dying disproportionately—people felt that this is bad, it should stop. And it seemed so sudden in some people's minds because media coverage suddenly begins or expands, and there is a momentariness to the attention.

This kind of momentary response is a symptom of the myth that you're speaking about—that Israel is a democratic, progressive state. Because the reality is that violence is the status quo, violence is everyday. It is normalized. The prevention of movement, the random arrests, the refusal to release people and bodies to families, the raids on people's homes, the killings, the evictions—these happen every day and not a single word is spoken about them.

So the airstrikes aren't actually an aberration, even though they come to be understood that way in people's minds. We see similar things happening here, like when the Grenfell Tower fire happens, when the Windrush scandal happens—people see these as an aberration when really the norm is a long history of colonial violence. And so the way in which this conflictual nature gets attached to Israel/Palestine is also a symptom of this myth that surrounds the situation. To speak of "conflict" and "unrest" suggests that there is rest and peace outside of that situation, which we know has not been the case in Israel since 1948 and before. Unless we recognize the reality and reject the myth, I don't think we can move toward a situation of solidarity. Where we don't understand the Palestinian struggle for liberation as a humanitarian one alone, as one that deserves our charity, our pity, and our compassion. But one which foregrounds the fact that this is a people struggling against apartheid, against settler colonialism—and recognizes Palestinians as empowered, purposive peoples with desires and goals of their own, and as being completely invested and engaged in the project of their own liberation in that context.

ILAN PAPPÉ: Yes, I totally agree. I find your book helpful because an important layer in the Israeli propaganda shield is creating a distinction between the occupied West Bank, the Gaza Strip, and Israel proper. In which Israel says, "We have Palestinians, but they are equal citizens—they can vote and elect the Palestinian minority in Israel." This alleged equal citizenship offered to the '48 Arabs, the Palestinian minority in Israel, shields Israel from international condemnation as a rogue and apartheid state.

I am also reminded of the way that Palestinian citizens of Israel are treated as and compared to immigrants, while Israel actually immigrated into their lives and homeland. Both the former subjects of the British Empire who immigrated to Britain (who are citizens by right) and the Palestinians to whose country Israel immigrated are not easily recognized as victims of colonization—because allegedly they are equal before the law. What emerges from your work is that, contrary to the liberal Zionist claim that the law in Israel protects Palestinian citizens from abusive and violent policies, in truth the law itself is an important part of the violence directed toward non-Jews. Or in the case of Britain, nonwhites. We must unpack the liberal language of equality in both contexts.

Let us move to a more general theme. *(B)ordering Britain* begins with reference to our beautiful city of Exeter, and your family history is connected to our Institute. Your parents arrived in Exeter in 1978 and, like all of us, were taken by the serenity of this city and the beauty of its surroundings. And yet there was a twist in the plot, which reminded me of what many Black students and people of color in the city experienced once the Leave campaign became active.

Your parents lived in the same suburb for forty years and when your father retired, his neighbor asked him if he would be going back to Egypt. You argue that the Leave campaign was not just a call to leave the EU, but also the old racist call for nonwhites to leave Britain. Later we will discuss how this kind of topology is maintained through discourse, law, and policies on the ground. But first let us speak in general terms, especially after the Windrush scandal[2] and the powerful appearance of Black Lives Matter impacted the discussion of Black Britain.

Unfortunately, the brave struggle of Black Britain and its brutal suppression in the 1970s and '80s was left out of that conversation.[3] Did these recent events and campaigns of awareness or recognition make you more sanguine about the way Britain, as a political system and as a society, is dealing with its imperial and colonial past and present? In particular, regarding the institutional racism and racialization embedded within Britain's legal system and immigration policies?

NADINE EL-ENANY: Of course the Black Lives Matter uprisings of 2020 gave me hope about the possibilities for a resistance movement in this country. I differentiate that from giving me hope about any kind of official response. It definitely lifted our spirits at a time when we were witnessing one of the most horrific impacts of a structurally and institutionally racist country like Britain. We were seeing and feeling that horror of the disproportionate deaths of racialized people as a result of the COVID-19 pandemic and the refusal of the government to do anything about this—to acknowledge that institutional racism in any way played a part. Instead they preferred to focus on underlying health conditions and comorbidities, taking a victim-blaming approach. But also they chose not to look at why health inequalities exist and why people working in certain sectors are disproportionately racialized and therefore disproportionately more exposed to the virus. We also saw the government adopting a situation of exceptionalism and a colonial logic of "surplus populations" who can be simply left to die.

So, yes, to see people rise up to be part of that movement gave me hope. I think it gave a lot of people hope and courage because we saw some amazing instances of solidarity and empowerment to speak about institutional racism. One of the things that stays with me is an action by the survivors and bereaved of the Grenfell Tower fire. I was so moved and so filled with hope to see them project the words "We can't breathe" onto Grenfell Tower. This was so powerful because it broke the silence about racism in relation to the Grenfell Tower fire, which has been at the core of the official response. The inquiry into the fire excludes the question of racism as being an issue in what happened. The fear among Grenfell residents of speaking out about this was really broken in that Black Lives Matter moment in the summer of 2020.

What also lifted me about that particular action is the way it allowed the issue of Black Lives Matter to gather an anti-imperialist global dimension in the message. It became a call that necessitated joining up of those who struggle against state and imperial racial oppression in all its forms, by projecting a call to justice being used in relation to the killings of Black people in the US onto a building in this domestic space of colonialism that is Britain. This can only make the movement stronger. In fact, I think it's the only way that the movement can succeed. So, in terms of the societal response, I would definitely say that especially after COVID-19 and the EU Referendum, with its effect of amplifying anti-migrant hysteria and racist hate, Black Lives Matter was an amazingly powerful moment.

But does it make me more sanguine about Britain as a political system dealing with its imperial and colonial past? I can't say that it does. There have been slight shifts in official discourse in the immediate aftermath, a kind of willingness to maybe take down a statue or two, but actually reneging on that as we've seen with Oxford and Rhodes recently.[4] Since then, we can look at examples of how the state responds in a very typically harsh way toward these protests. One is the Police Crime, Sentencing, and Courts bill, which provoked the amazing Kill the Bill demonstrations.[5] But we know that this bill was introduced in response to the strength of the street movements we are talking about. It *has* been the target of this amazing resistance in cities across the country. It also seems to have seen the emergence of what is relatively unprecedented in recent decades: a coalitional resistance by all the communities targeted by the bill, like those campaigning against violence against women, migrant organizations, gypsy and traveller groups, those affected by school suspensions, people campaigning against police brutality, stop and search. They are all coming together to resist this bill. Black Lives Matter of the summer of 2020 will also have made those demonstrations against the bill possible.

But the bill is also clearly a nod to the Tory, white, propertied voting base, reassuring them not to worry about civil unrest: "We've got your backs, we're going to protect your interests." The other example that makes me less hopeful about the official response is the Sewell report—the government's appointed Commission on Race and Ethnic Disparities.[6] This comes during a time when we have seen some of the most horrific effects of structural racism, and the intersection between race and class in this country with the disproportionate deaths resulting from the pandemic. Also, on the heels of the BLM [Black Lives Matter] uprisings, the report makes the claim that there is no institutional racism in Britain—a complete denial that institutional racism exists. The Sewell report presents institutional racism as a figment of the "warped mentality" of Black and Brown people. It states that calls to address racism are part of "youthful idealism" and actually work to obscure the urgent needs of a left-behind white working class, who are neglected by these elite multiculturalists.

In that sense, I don't have hope in this kind of official response. But what gives me hope is the movements emerging in response to state racism in terms of Kill the Bill. But also the amazing solidarity with Palestine—these are the biggest demonstrations in support of Palestine in the history of this country. They have been absolutely amazing. This movement is growing and of course it is causing consternation—and there are attempts to suppress it.

The irony of the Sewell report is that it criticized a really maligned "BAME" label—Black, Asian, and minority ethnic. The report claims that the label holds together a group that in truth is not a community, and that this is somehow insulting to racialized people. But this is ironic because the report tries to deny a solidarity that we actually see as existing in the form of Kill the Bill, the Free Palestine movement, and the demonstrations we've seen. It is precisely a coalitional solidaristic movement—people recognizing their bonds with each other, resisting attempts to divide us along lines of identity, and realizing our connectedness. And the connectedness of the struggles against state violence.

ILAN PAPPÉ: Let's talk about the potential of human rights work that lawyers are doing in this country, which you refer to in your work. A few days ago, I met a lawyer representing one of the families evicted from the Sheikh Jarrah neighborhood in Jerusalem. He said to me, "This is some of the most depressing work I'm doing." When I asked why, he replied, "Even if we succeed, which I doubt, I am helping this family to stay in an oppressed apartheid neighborhood and to continue living with the danger of a future ethnic cleansing. It's not as if I am going to court and if we succeed, it will dramatically transform the life of my clients."

An important part of your work is an engagement with the politics of recognition, with particular interest in how it affects the defense work done by lawyers on behalf of those defined as refugees, aliens, and immigrants. While you believe that a critical approach to the politics of recognition in settler-colonial studies, which many of our students work with, is progressing and having an impact, you cannot say the same for those who practice and teach human rights law in Britain. This means that while it may be important to fight for the rights of Black, Brown, and so-called non-white people, who are former subjects or citizens of the Empire, to receive the status of citizenship or any statutory rights, the contemporary racial and colonial nature of Britain "does not alter the way in which racialized people are cast in white spaces as undeserving guests, outsiders, or intruders." I quote your book directly here. This is something that "nonwhite" students in our university—and really all universities—are fully aware of, for instance, when exposed to racist abuse in the city and on campus. To demonstrate this deficiency, you pointed to the struggle of those victimized by the Windrush scandal, and their legal representatives, when it was clear that public discourse did not acknowledge that Britain owes its affluence to the spoils of colonialism—which were then denied to former citizens and subjects, among them those who arrived during the 1940s.

To counter this, you offer an alternative—a "counter-pedagogy" that is absent from the work of human rights lawyers striving to help their clients achieve recognition. Can you explain what you mean by this?

NADINE EL-ENANY: It comes back to myths and the need to challenge them. I speak of a counter-pedagogy specifically against the hegemonic reading that law gives us. Laws passed in the '60s, '70s, and '80s constructed Britain as a postimperial space through the use of an invented legal concept called "patriality." This essentially said that in 1971, unless you were a person born in Britain or had a parent born in Britain, you did not have the right to enter and remain in Britain. In 1971, a person born in Britain was 98 percent likely to be white. It's very clear what was being written into the law.

The effect was essentially racial exclusion—the severing of connections to Britain, the right to enter and remain for former colonial and Commonwealth citizens. This had a powerful material effect, but also a powerful symbolic effect in constructing Britain as a postimperial, legitimately bordered, sovereign nation-state. What I say is that working with the law is obviously important for lawyers like the person representing the Sheikh Jarrah families. We need law in those urgent moments! But law won't help us to achieve our long-term radical goals for transformation and justice. We need to be aware that every time we use the colonial state's law as legal practitioners and legal scholars, we also reinforce its authority to *determine* who has access to Britain and the spoils of empire, who has the right to ownership of land in Palestine.

There are many parallels to draw, but what's happening is a reinforcing of power and an erasure of colonial history. It is so important to contextualize these laws in a way that demonstrates why they are unjust, why they should be seen as instances of colonial violence. The laws are not some neutral thing that does the work of "justice" by dividing the deserving from the undeserving on the basis of what are neutral categories.

The book is an attempt to provide a counter-pedagogy and a counternarrative, which places laws in their proper historical context. But I also make the argument that if we look at the laws themselves in their proper historical context and then understand them as racial violence, then we also should understand an irregularized migrant—activity that is criminalized—as being something else. As being anticolonial resistance because the laws that are being breached or obstructed are themselves instances of colonial violence. It's a whole reframing of how we think about law and how we think about resistance and breakages of the law.

I am careful that when I say "irregularized migration is anticolonial resistance," I'm not promoting it—for the reason that it's such a dangerous thing to do. The hostile environments that people are subjected to pre- and post-arrival are murderous. But what I am saying is that it is precisely the illegality in the activity—the forcible defiance of the laws that are designed to obstruct the restoration of colonial property, the relationship of illegality and forced redistribution—that actually gives irregularized migration its anticolonial dimension. So it's a counternarrative that insists on a recognition that the story of Britain's making is fiction. But it also has an important psychic dimension. Because what happens is that, rather than understanding themselves as rightfully at the mercy of law and legal status recognition processes, racialized people living within a colonial space see themselves as collectively entitled to resist their oppression. To reclaim their wealth, their land, what was stolen from them. As entitled to presence, freedom of movement, equality, and justice.

ILAN PAPPÉ: Those who are familiar with (B)ordering Britain know that it is also about ordering Britain. In your activism and writing, you engage with identifying how the state frames public order and disorder through a depoliticized criminalization of political dissent, which is motivated by a clear political agenda. I was amazed to learn how rulings, acts, and policies of kettling, charging through a body of demonstrators with horses, and other brutal means were all historically legitimized. And they continue to be legitimized with more or less the same reasoning from the late nineteenth century onward.

Am I going too far if I include the Prevent program as another illumination of ordering Britain? Is it part of the same methodology? And how can we challenge these unacceptable restrictions on our freedoms?

NADINE EL-ENANY: Well, it's not just a program. Prevent is also a legal duty placed on public bodies to prevent people from being drawn into terrorism.[7] And it does come with a whole program, including requirements for training people. But this legal duty has had serious effects in relation to academic freedom, as you mention. I don't think it is going too far to include Prevent and a long history of suppression and criminalization of dissent in ordering Britain. Controlling racially and economically oppressed populations has always required a system of surveillance, alongside brutal forms of policing on the street. These systems have also often included drawing so-called ordinary citizens, employers, teachers into this surveillance system, which is the work of the state. By law, the Counter-Terrorism and Security Act of 2015 introduced the duty of universities to take action to prevent people being drawn into terrorism.[8]

We know the political context—the Islamophobic context, the anti-Muslim racist context—in which these laws are introduced. And so we know the people who are targeted as a result of laws like this, which might masquerade as pertaining to all forms of extremism. The very vague guidance issued alongside this law leaves a lot of scope for misuse of this duty. We see it in our own workplaces, in universities for example. It's not just the law that is applied—they often have very overzealous interpretations of the law, which make us all complicit in state racism. In recent weeks here in the UK we've seen Prevent used to target school students who are speaking out in support of Palestine or just wearing Palestine badges. Trying to raise awareness at school, they face the full force of the school's disciplinary mechanisms—all under the guise of Prevent.

Teachers are misinformed about the Palestinian struggle because they are taught in training programs that demonstrating any kind of support for Palestine is a sign of being drawn into extremism. The Prevent program also allows preexisting prejudices to then be enacted against Muslim students. And we've seen that in our own institutions. It's not just the Prevent program, it's also how international students are treated. They are hounded by university administrations who are terrified of falling foul of the Home Office, which again brings in the bordering aspect. We have discriminatory registration requirements and universities going above and beyond in their differential treatment of international students. And we are all complicit in this! I never expected to be a border guard, considering the kind of work that I do. But I absolutely am, in the kind of registration that I have to subject my students to.

I worry about Prevent in the ways we are talking about because of how it legitimizes control, punishment, and criminalization. But it also has a self-policing effect as people become afraid to do the kind of research that they want, or speak out in public forums in case they are accused of breaching legal duties—falling foul of the Prevent program. If the state doesn't succeed in silencing you, you end up silencing yourself.

In terms of how we challenge these things, we need to try to not be complicit as much as we possibly can. The place to start is our workplaces and our own departments—and making sure that we refuse, as far as possible, everything that comes with the Prevent duty. We need to make our colleagues aware of the harms that result from these kinds of obligations. We need to support our students in still having their pro-Palestine events and their ability to speak out in class. There is also work being done within our unions in terms of training people in how to resist Prevent.

ILAN PAPPÉ: As an activist and scholar, you were also very much involved in the aftermath of the Grenfell Tower fire, in which seventy-two people lost their lives on June 14, 2017. You edited a book with Dan Bulley and Jenny Edkins titled *After Grenfell: Violence, Resistance and Response.* This book exposes the fire as a criminal act born of neoliberal economics, the racialization of subjects, and the denial of basic rights to those who either do not have the status of citizens, or those who have citizenship but are excluded from receiving adequate housing. This reality was accentuated by the inadequate responses from the government and local council to the fire and the loss of life and property. No less important, we are left with knowledge that oppressive economic policies coupled with immigration and citizenship laws leave many more towers as potential infernos in the future.

The book also talks about resistance. Is this a resistance based on future solidarity between the groups that are the focus of your work? People who are racialized as "nonwhite" in Britain organizing with whites (the working class) who are seemingly not affected by citizenship or immigration laws, but by austerity, neoliberalism, and the legacies of a class-based society. You frame the trajectory of a pillage of spoils, highlighting the affluence built on it and the denial of access to it. This raises the question: Where are the whites who are also denied access to this affluence? In a way, they belong to the community of robbers but do not have a share in the spoils.

I'm intrigued by this because it reminds me of how Arab Jews, the Mizrahi Jews, still struggle today to get a larger share of the land robbed from the Palestinians in 1948. It is a question of social justice. They deserve more land, but this land was dispossessed from the Palestinians who inhabited it or were made refugees. In the case of the Arab Jews, this is a marginalized social and ethnic group within the settler society, which despite its attempts to de-Arabize itself is not treated as equal to the European Jews.

Are you interested in such an alliance in Britain, politically? How do you value its importance and prospects?

NADINE EL-ENANY: Yes, I absolutely see the resistance that we urgently need now as being coalitional. As bringing together all those dispossessed by intersecting oppressive forces, whether colonialism, racism, or neoliberalism. To my mind, this is the only kind of resistance that has a chance of righting some of history's wrongs—

of seeing a redistribution of wealth and resources, of seeing that everyone has a chance to flourish and to thrive, not just survive. But I sometimes fear that we are far from this kind of coalitional form of solidarity.

We can find ourselves embroiled in arguments within resistance movements about who can use a slogan or who can use a particular term. We saw this in the wake of BLM in 2020. Can we say Brown Lives Matter? Or can we only say that Black Lives Matter? Can we say Palestinian Lives Matter? This hoarding of words can be quite unhelpful. It can be an attachment to victimhood, and a failure to envision and then fight for a future in which attachments to identity begin to fall away. What we're striving for is an equal society in which people are not mistreated or dehumanized on account of their differences. A world in which these kinds of differences and the way they matter now actually cease to matter. So we cannot say that the person can only be part of a movement if they are racialized.

What we want is a movement that works toward a place in time where it doesn't matter if one is racialized or not for the chance to live, to thrive in society. I would want a kind of solidarity in which material, social, cultural, racial, and other differences do not prohibit coalition. They are acknowledged as important in placing us and our experiences, and the differential way in which oppression affects us in terms of how we're racialized through material conditions. But this can nevertheless be a solidaristic movement where we reach across these differences and divides toward meeting. I always come back to this quote from Hélène Cixous: we search for "people who are like [us] in their rebellion and in their hope."[9] Because, for me, this is the most important thing. If we have that in common then we can come together. Then we can embrace.

It requires embracing the complex, messy work of organizing. It's never going to be clean and easy to organize and struggle together.

It's always going to be an embracing of complexity—the pain of that, the confusion of that, the challenging of our own assumptions, our own entitlement, our own guilt, our own shame. All of the messiness of what it means to be human. And then you confront that—you embrace it and you wade through that messiness. That's how you build this truly solidaristic kind of movement. And I also think that I am no more fit for the struggle because I am a racialized person, because I have experienced racism. I really believe I'm no more fit for this struggle in lots of ways than the child of the colonizer who witnesses the injustices around them and joins their brothers and sisters in the struggle against oppression. I really think that. And that's what makes the movement stronger, in recognizing that. And finding each other in how we are like each other "in our rebellion and in our hope."

ILAN PAPPÉ: Thank you, Nadine. This was so important for all of us. In my last question, I want to go back to Palestine, the politics of recognition, and international law. When you write about the problems of the politics of recognition, you also extend your discussion to other parts of the world—in particular to the struggles of Indigenous people in places such as Canada and Australia. The questions you tap into are very relevant to the discussion among Palestinians and those who support their struggle. You raise questions about the relevance of international law, including international human rights law, to the struggle for freedom and justice. Britain is a colonial space, and so is Israel. What does it tell us about the relevance or irrelevance of international law to Palestine?

Some scholars, such as Noura Erakat, go even further and warn us that international law provides a liberal global shield that helps to perpetuate colonization rather than challenging it. Can engaging with international law be done within what you called "counter-pedagogy," which you explained to us as a new framing? Would it require us to understand the historical context in which international law was born? As you remind us again and again, laws are not born out of the blue. The historical context here is the way that settler-colonial societies and states were able to shield themselves from being judged by international law, by not allowing the law in the '60s to define settler colonialism as colonialism.

I was very surprised to read about how Canada, the United States, and other countries were making sure that while colonialism would be condemned by international law, settler colonialism would not be part of that discussion. This historical exclusion later generated the poignant critique directed by Indigenous movements toward international law. If I can conclude and summarize this point, how do you see the relevance of international law for the struggle for justice in Palestine and other settler-colonial settings where Indigenous people are not recognized in international law?

NADINE EL-ENANY: I'm not an expert on international law, but there are many excellent, critical international law scholars who have shown through careful historical excavation and analysis how international law serves to enshrine the colonial order and global racial hierarchy in myriad ways and fields over the past decades. I'll just take, for example, international human rights law, which I write about in the book. Human rights are enshrined in so many international and regional treaties and domestic legal systems. The problem is, are we even sure that we agree on who or what constitutes a human being? Can we say for certain that we're talking about the same thing when we say "human"? I don't think so. If we agreed on what the term "human" meant, I don't think that we would see the mass racial violence and murder and corresponding impunity—its total lack of registration, of even computing, as violence in so many minds.

I'm thinking, of course, of Palestine. I'm thinking of the invasion in Iraq. I'm thinking of the Grenfell Tower fire. All of the things we've been talking about today. We know that colonialism and white supremacy necessitate the dehumanization of people. And they've long done the work of shaping psyches, so that many people are unable to register as *violence* something that happens to a Brown person, a Black person, a Muslim person. I often ask myself this question in relation to Iraq: How can millions die due to this invasion, and it does not register as unacceptable?

And then we see the Grenfell Tower fire. We see the images of the victims, the vast majority of whom are Muslim. People have become so accustomed to seeing people in headscarves and with brown faces as being the victims of violence. The violence that they experience is so normalized it doesn't register as being in any way remarkable. When you say that this cladding remains on so many buildings—had the fire happened in a building with predominantly white people, it's possible that that would have registered as violence. And that something would have happened to at least take the cladding off a similar building.

Human rights law also plays a role in obscuring state racism. And by obscuring state racism, we don't see what it is that we actually need to tackle. If we think about human rights and antidiscrimination law, they're kind of soft signifiers for racism. Racism becomes constructed as an aberration from legal norms as perpetuated by an individual, rather than something structurally produced and sustained through law. But of course, human rights law is both useful and useless in urgent situations. People facing the violence of the law—being deported, having their home under threat—go to the law because it's the last resort. But if we think about migration law for a moment, individuals only come within the protection of human rights law when they fall within the jurisdiction of the state. And that's why we see so many people dying at sea. Because the state does everything it possibly can to ensure that people never make it into the jurisdiction of the state, and lose their lives in the process of trying.

Looking for hope in international human rights is understandable and it can sometimes be found—but it's always going to be in the form of incremental change. We won't be talking in terms of abolition, liberation, or transformation if we are looking to international law. I think it does make a difference because of course it matters which government is in power and which laws are in place for individuals seeking family reunification, asylum, naturalization. The specific laws in place matter. Therefore a more reformist struggle is necessary alongside, keeping in mind our radical goals.

We can look at it in the context of Palestine and the International Criminal Court's (ICC) declaration that it will investigate Israel for war crimes.[10] At the time, lawyers hoped that this was going to make a difference because individual Israeli soldiers might fear prosecution, might fear traveling abroad—they might think twice about their actions. But then we see the status quo and the recent military action in spite of this recent declaration. I don't think there are any reports from Palestinians on the ground that this declaration has somehow changed the everyday brutality they face, including shoot-to-kill and shoot-to-blind policies. There is no report that these kinds of international legal machinations actually make a difference in their daily lives.

What they might do is contribute to the sense of a shift, a sea change in a growing unwillingness on the ground—in movements of people coming together who reject this total impunity on the part of the Israeli government and the military—and reinforce a grass-roots resistance. If we're talking about radical change, that's the kind of campaign we need. A campaign where people, including those within institutions who bring their institutions on board, make the situation in Palestine and its system of policies too costly to be sustained. That's the kind of pressure that is needed.

We've been here before with histories of movements against colonialism and we can learn from these histories—how to organize and how to bring people together. For me, there is some necessity in paying attention to the law and using it when necessary. But also always focusing on how to build movements and connections with each other. One of the things I always take hope from, whilst the state is always trying to break bonds, to divide, to oppress, to exert its rule, its violence, is that in moments of crisis, we see people coming together.

And one of the things I particularly take hope from is the way in which mutual aid groups were formed in Britain, for example, in the midst of the pandemic. The state moved quickly to try to co-opt these groups, but it didn't work. It was a failed attempt. What actually happened is that people who lived on the same streets, who lived in neighborhoods, who may have never spoken before, came together and practically supported each other. These are bonds of care, bonds of love, bonds of defiance against the state's willful neglect and failure. And these are the bonds that can't be broken.

Paul Gilroy

HISTORIES FOR THE FUTURE

June 10, 2021

Professor of the Humanities Paul Gilroy, the founding director of the Sarah Parker Remond Centre for the Study of Racism and Racialisation at University College London, is one of the foremost theorists of race and racism working and teaching in the world today. He is the author of foundational and highly influential books such as *There Ain't No Black in the Union Jack* (1987), *The Black Atlantic: Modernity and Double Consciousness* (1993), *Against Race: Imagining Political Culture beyond the Color Line* (2000), *Postcolonial Melancholia* (2005), and *Darker than Blue: On the Moral Economies of Black Atlantic Culture* (2010) alongside numerous key articles, essays, and critical interventions. Gilroy's is a unique voice that speaks to the centrality and tenacity of racialized thought and representational practices in the modern world. Winner of the Holberg Prize (2019), which is given to a person who has made outstanding contributions to research in the arts, humanities, social science, the law, or theology, Professor Gilroy was described by the awarding committee as "one of the most challenging and inventive figures in contemporary scholarship." Gilroy was one of the founding figures of a remapped global history that embedded the movement of racialized subjects and traded goods into accounts of the world as we know it. His work on racism in modern Britain has consistently countered romantic narratives of whiteness, Christianity, and ethnic homogeneity as uniquely constitutive of these islands and has written the long history of Black Britons into the cultural and social fabric of Britishness.

ILAN PAPPÉ: Thank you again for joining us, Paul. What I will try and do is take some, as it is impossible to take all, of your rich intellectual contributions over the years as a framework and methodology for discussing the present and future in Britain and Palestine. I grouped our concerns into three major questions, based on my understanding of the methodology one can carve out of your works, which is extremely useful in analyzing and facing racism in Britain and beyond, and settler colonialism in Palestine and beyond.

The methodology has three elements as I see it, almost a tool kit for the future scholar, especially the younger generation. You offer three new genealogies: of racism, the struggle against it, and the role of academia in sustaining racism and in opposing it.

The first two issues are the more crucial ones. You suggest that the best way to analyze contemporary racism (and by inference, fascism) and settler colonialism is by revising the genealogy of the brutality incurred in present-day racism and settler colonialism and the struggle against them. Through such a genealogy we might ask how racism produced "race" and settler colonialism produced what you call "infrahumanity," or dehumanization. When we search for a new genealogy of the struggle against racism, we ask two questions. First, why was it never a central part of the Western struggle for human rights? And second, where it *was* part of such a struggle in recent years, what are its limitations? As you fear, it seems to be a superficial struggle and sometimes ineffective, if not inadvertently perpetuating racism and neofascism.

These questions are all interconnected. I do not think we can or should separate our discussion of the genealogy of racism from the search for human rights. Within this genealogical frame we should explore whether the struggle coexisted with racism, interacted with it; we should examine whether the selection of who was included or excluded from the journey in the search to protect human rights was based itself on racism, and what hybridities and fallacies both racism and the struggle against it produced. This fusion is needed for viewing the discourse on human rights after the Second World War, which was influenced by the Holocaust and is needed if we want to include Palestine in the conversation. It seems to me that while these rereadings included the Holocaust, but not genocides of Africans or Muslims in Southeast Asia, they also left out the Nakba—and because of that the journey and its rereading are incomplete and deficient to a certain degree.

So, my first question is about retelling the history of human rights discourses and approaches in the West and their relevance to Palestine. In the genealogy that you chart, the Treaty of Utrecht,[1] the American Declaration of the Rights and Duties of Man,[2] and the United Nations Universal Declaration of Human Rights[3] are all stations in a Western trajectory that selectively pushed forward an "enlightened" agenda, which allowed "nonenlightened" ideas to flourish outside the continent of Europe in its colonized spaces. This agenda created categories of humanity and infrahumanity "over there" and excluded, even in 1948, identifying racism as a major obstacle in our quest to protect human rights.

When you revisited this journey, you found that Africans and people of the Caribbean, within the West and outside of it, wished to be part of the conversation but in most cases were silenced or ignored. Such was the case of Antoine Frangulis, the representative of Haiti in the League of Nations, who in 1933 called for an international conference on human rights and racism in response to the Nazi anti-Jewish policies. But his voice was stifled by the American delegation, which did not wish to discuss the racist laws and practices in the USA together with the anti-Jewish laws of Germany at the time. This is very much as today, when President Biden does not want the ICC to investigate Israel, as it might investigate the US and its allies.

This was around the same time Mahatma Gandhi wrote to Martin Buber explaining that he would never support Zionism, as the Jewish settlers came not to live alongside the native Palestinian population but to replace them. His warning was also ignored. Thus, alongside the genocide of the Jews in Europe, the world also witnessed the ethnic cleansing of the Palestinians. And we can add James Baldwin's perceptive observation that the Palestinians would be victim of an antisemitic wish to see the Jews expelled from the West and serving British colonial interests in the East.

This new reading also raises intriguing questions about a Declaration of Human Rights in 1948, which was drafted when most of the world was still colonized and was only, or perhaps primarily, triggered because Europeans perpetrated genocide against other Europeans. The genocide of Africans by Europeans did not produce in the West any need for such a declaration. Years later, when George Mosse attributed Nazi dehumanization to the blunt indifference toward inhumanity in the First World War, no one attributed it to the slave trade, the Belgian genocide in Congo, or the Italian genocide in Libya. And as you mention in your work, very few connected the Nazi horrors to the use of mustard gas by the Italians in Ethiopia.

And here is where I would like to introduce Palestine. Some of your protagonists, who are obvious heroes in creating a different genealogy, are survivors of the Holocaust who aligned their analyses of the horror they personally experienced with the evil of colonization. One such person is Jean Améry, who read [Frantz] Fanon while being tortured by the Nazis. And yet that same incredible person whom I admired was an ardent supporter of the state of Israel—after, it should be said, the Nakba, a crime against humanity perpetrated by a state pretending to represent the victims of the Holocaust.

Primo Levi, another inspirational hero in this respect, waited until 1982 to voice the first criticism of Israel and paid dearly by being shunned by the Italian and American Jewish communities. These Zionist Jews refused to accept a concept or a possibility of Jewish racism, even from Primo Levi. And when I—whose parents lost most of their family in the Holocaust—claim that racism is at the heart of Israeli oppression of the Palestinians, which includes torture, ethnic cleansing, and genocidal policies, I could be branded if not sued as antisemitic or otherwise an incurable self-hating Jew. This is according to the new definition of Holocaust denial, which unfortunately my university adopted—the infamous IHRA definition.

I would like to include the racism of Zionism within this new reading and enter into your genealogy Hajo Meyer and Gabor Maté, whose experiences in the Holocaust led them to accuse Zionism of racism (in the name of their experience) and reject the exceptionalism granted to that form of racism by some of the most honorable fighters against racism elsewhere. Zionism is and was a brand of racism easily understood by the African member states in the UN when they helped to pass the 1975 resolution equating Zionism with racism. Can we say that the analysis and stances of both Améry and Levi were profoundly deficient for not including the Palestinian story in the struggle, and will we not err ourselves as well if we exclude Palestinian suffering at the hands of Zionist racism from the new genealogy? Do forgive me for this long preface, but I wanted to bring it all together, as this is also a personal experience and interest, and not just an intellectual quest for knowledge.

PAUL GILROY: Thank you for less a question and more of a survey, from which it is difficult to dissent. I don't know how to begin to answer you, because it is so obviously the case that you've outlined. The core of your question seems to me: Why hasn't the struggle against racism been part of the Western pursuit of human rights? And secondly, why hasn't the Nakba—the suffering, the injustice, the structural and systematic inequalities, and the violence directed against Palestinians—been able to enter that story? There are a number of difficult answers to those questions that would detain us for the entire evening.

Why isn't the struggle against racism part of the Western pursuit of human rights? I think it's because of the way that "the human" in human rights has been configured. That's my point of entry. You mentioned early on that I spoke about infrahumanism and planetary humanism—I think these are my own profoundly deficient attempts to complicate our understanding of the human in pursuit of human rights. And to suggest elements of an alternative genealogy. I think it isn't any problem to see how the story of Palestinian expropriation, of colonial violence in Palestine, might be folded into that story very readily.

In his introduction to our talk, Malcolm Richards was kind enough to mention that I had been involved in producing a photographic history of Black life in Britain. One of the photographs in that book is from the Pan-African Conference of 1945, prior to the establishment of the state of Israel. And as the speaker from the international Labor party approaches the rostrum to address this conference—which I believe is the first where non-US voices are dominant amongst the organizing group—there's a placard on the wall behind him. The placard says, "Jews and Arabs unite against British imperialism."

It was important to me to include that because when I first found the photograph, I was struck by how seldom I had seen that pronouncement made. And I was struck that in the immediate aftermath of World War II, such a statement was at the center of a pan-African meeting. Some years ago I had the pleasure of being involved in a project around the representations of the British Empire on film. Apart from seeing General Allenby's forces marching into Jerusalem, we were able to look at the two different versions of the post-1945 victory parade that were enacted on celluloid for benefit of celebrants of the empire. The first version, for the consumption of domestic audiences in England, included no colonial troops. The second version included all the imperial and colonial forces, including a significant contingent of Palestinian soldiers in uniform marching down the mall.

Now, obviously my work is unified by its distaste and opposition to nationalism in all forms. So I'm not being a crypto-nationalist to say that I'm attached to England profoundly. But I think that a large part of the answer to your question relates to the residual force and presence of the British Empire in the world. If you were to show the film with Palestinian soldiers in British colonial army uniforms from 1945 marching through London, there would be a great shock to see this. And I don't think we can underestimate the deficit of historical knowledge, which is available to us, in drawing intellectual energy and attention to the kind of counter-genealogy you described.

That's the first thing I'd say: history and the British Empire. And the second thing relates to the force of the colonial double standard, the colonial *nomos*. In my work, I've tried to take it back to seventeenth-century sources, which are fundamental to the development of political theory. In particular, I've tried to read the *Second Treatise of Government*[4] with this question in mind. In the context of the colonial dynamics of the establishment of Israel and its legitimation, we see the colonial doctrine of improving the land—which requires improvement and where supposedly the Indigenous people sacrifice their title to that land, their relation to that land, and are opening themselves to expropriation from that land by their failure to improve it.

In Locke's original arguments, this is already doubly coded—because it says to the emergent revolutionary force of the bourgeoisie, "You can take what you like in this colonial world." And perhaps in the hub of empire, this is a revolutionary clarion call to the bourgeoisie as it emerges onto the stage of world history. But in the colonial zone, this is a license for murder, a license for horror, a license for violence. So it's really trying to capture that double standard that is intrinsic to the, and I am quoting someone, "peculiarly English way of thinking"—about land, about identity, about property. This is something that comes out of the center of the English Revolution in the seventeenth century and is applied viciously and brutally to Ireland, the first colony of England.

I want to suggest that there are key ambiguities in these ways of thinking about land, property, belonging, and revolutionary transformation in the doctrine of improvement, which is affirmed and maintained by successes that warrant the colonial domination of the world and the expropriation of Indigenous peoples, wherever the life and machinery of the British Empire touches their experience. Those ambiguities are retained. I want to direct people toward that, too.

Now a third thing: there is something about the intellectual and political confrontation with racism itself that promotes a certain, at worst, agonistic relationship with the categories of humanity. This is what I'm trying to get at through the concept of "planetary humanism," which is derived from a reading of [Aimé] Césaire in the late 1940s. Césaire speaks about a humanism "made the measure of the world"—not a European universalism alone, but something that we can now begin to recognize in the postglobalism engagement with our planetary lives that's been underscored by the pandemic.

There is a new set of questions about what humanist discourses need to be in the future, in our assessments of risk, vulnerability, and sustainability. This is also something that comes across very strongly in the most exciting and urgent writing that has emerged in the face of the climate crisis. There are new ways of being human at stake. If we are scholars, if we are academics, then what we study and what we research corresponds to what we are in some way. I don't know exactly how, but I know that that horizon is very important to me.

Specifically on the question of Palestine, I don't know where to begin to narrate my own personal story, but I will say that I have always been greatly guided by Edward Said. I remember reading *Orientalism* in 1978 when it was first published and thinking about how one might begin to integrate a concern with the projection of the Orient as an object of knowledge and power into a larger framework of critical commentary on racial hierarchy, racialized forms of injustice, racialized forms of violence, and so on. I'm very indebted to Edward for opening that window for me. But he's certainly not the only person and not the only experience of that.

In my own life, the invasion of Lebanon in the early 1980s was a very important and formative experience for me in trying to think about this again. And here, my teacher was the African American poet and writer June Jordan. She was the person who instructed me, informed me, and educated me as to how that concern, that openness, that attachment to the struggles of Palestinian people could be interwoven, interlaced, or productively entangled with the kinds of things that were emerging in my own work at that point. Many people will understand her voice as a Black feminist voice that was ecumenical, universalist, strongly humanist in some ways, always modest. During that period, she wrote a very famous poem of apology to the Palestinian people—"Apologies to All the People in Lebanon"—and a whole sequence of poems when she went to Lebanon in the aftermath of those events.[5] I could say a lot more about my practice in the classroom and who I've learned from. Edward used to talk about [Martin] Buber and the Buber family taking his own family's house. I think this question of being drawn toward Buber and the *I and Thou*—seeing a fantastic resource for managing the responsibility that we bear in the face of the other—was for me rather undermined when I heard Edward Said speak about the Buber family. The case of [Emmanuel] Levinas is equally well known. The inability to distinguish the abstract alterity from the concrete alterity in Levinas's beautiful biblical system. So important, so useful—and yet, so limited.

So I want to suggest that where you say that this work is "profoundly deficient," I agree with you. But I think its deficiencies are instructive. I think its deficiencies are stimulating and urgent and provocative. Because I know how deficient my own work is, I don't search for perfection. I embrace those deficiencies and hopefully allow myself to be stimulated by them further. In each of those cases, this has become useful to me in directing me to the place where that double standard is most intensely present. And it seems to me that that double standard *is* racism. That double standard is the colonial *nomos*. That double standard is its fundamental characteristic.

ILAN PAPPÉ: You just reminded me that one of the last conversations I had with Edward Said before he died was about the contradiction between what he wrote in general about nationalism, how he deconstructed it, and what he wrote on Palestinian nationalism. He said to me, "You know, I came to the conclusion that paradoxes can be left. They don't have to be resolved. I don't have to explain it." There is something there to think about in line with what you said.

I would like to talk more about national liberation movements, which are still under the colonial yoke today—not a closed chapter from the past—and how much can we and should we humanize and transnationalize the culture of liberatory movements when they are in the midst of struggling against colonization. This has a lot to do with the way you offer us a fresh way of unpacking decolonization, which for you is incomplete if racism is not tackled head-on as a principal component in the analysis. You do this by rereading decolonization as the long story of individual agency of the colonized and the enslaved, and by blurring the relationship between the colonial worlds and their victims. Maybe the photograph you mentioned is one such instance. Here, ships did not just carry slaves, but also people who refused to be slaves and inhabited maritime routes that allow the exchange of culture (as well as people) in a way that created a hybrid and transnational culture, which is a far cry from the way it was later dogmatized and nationalized on the territorial basis.

This forced you, I feel, to be not just a historian, but also a DJ, a curator, and a collector—so that ordinary agency and human exchange would challenge the Manichaean view of human relationship and identities, as well as racist realties. You managed to reveal conviviality in the past as an inspirational model for the future. You archived knowledge in the quest to avoid the melancholy that some famous archaeologists of knowledge cast in their histories and genealogies of knowledge.

This corresponds to some new and exciting works that recently appeared on Palestine and the Arab world. One of them,

The Ecumenical Frame by Ussama Makdisi, shows a past where collective identities were not insisted upon. This tallies with what you said about the Palestinians before imperial invasion. Today, these identities are what Orientalists and pundits in the West disparagingly call "sectarianism," and to which they attribute the current violence and brutality in the Arab world.

According to Makdisi, collective identities were a vague way of life that enabled coexistence in a genuine way—without, of course, idealizing or romanticizing the nature of the Ottoman Empire within which they lived. But more often than not it was less present in their lives than the modern state is in ours. This frame was destroyed mainly by Western imperialism, and in Palestine by Zionism.

In particular I was thinking of your rereading of *Uncle Tom's Cabin*, or the way you revisited English folk songs and their transmutations under the influence of African and Caribbean music, and the recovery of various instances that told us that we might be writing a history of slavery but not of slaves. Rather, these are people who did all they could not to be slaves, not to give up conviviality, even if at times they had to find it in a supranatural world of spirits and saints. So, it is about agency, but also about possibilities of hybridity and ordinary human interactions, even under oppression. A genealogy that opened the way to a history of women and gender, and maybe in some ways was opened by feminist historiography. Take out the historical circumstances and you have a cultural model for the future, which is transnational, universal, convivial, and ordinary. And maybe even one that can become an antidote to racism and fascism.

But Palestinians would ask: Can we skip the national liberation phase? Is this a scenario of a humanist culture that unfolds after you struggle for liberation, or should it be part of that struggle? You might find yourself muted in the face of your oppressor's brutality if you dwell on the humanist transnational culture while struggling to be free or to exist. But if you neglect this quest, you might wake up to the Fanonian nightmare of replacing the French tormentor with the tormentor of the liberation movement.

I just wonder whether envisioning and working toward transnational humanist culture can be done as part of a reconciliation process or only after it happens. As I am not Palestinian, I attempted to express this in a dialogue with my compatriots—my Jewish compatriots—in Israel. It resulted in a dismal failure, but I am not giving up. In 2005, a headline in an Israeli newspaper accused me of stirring hatred and animosity in a lecture at Tel Aviv University by referring to the Jews who came to Israel from Arab countries as "Arab Jews." I thought, maybe naively, that the fact that so many of the settlers come from a rich heritage of being not only Jews but also Arabs is a manifestation of how one can view culture as a vernacular, ordinary, and dynamic sphere of human activity. Rather than a signifier that, in case of the Jews who came from Arab countries, forced them to publicly denounce their Arabism, to de-Arabize themselves if they wanted to be part of the "whites" in the apartheid system that Israel built. As you can see from the reaction, in places where postcolonialism could only be a fantasy rather than an unfolding reality, colonialism and racism are still rife, even in the twenty-first century. And I wonder, could it be fought without identity politics as a transnational liberation movement rather than a national one?

How much should we strive to challenge a fantasy of purity, not only of the colonizer but also of the colonized? Is there a right timing for this, or is it imperative from the very start? I was once quite melancholic when despairing about our ability to arrest the quest for purity on both sides of the colonial and racist divide in Palestine and beyond, but I am much more sanguine based on what

I hear from younger Palestinians, who are the majority in their society and seem to endorse a universalist quest that does not negate a liberatory vision. A different way of asking this is: What is decolonization really in the twenty-first century, and in particular in places such as Palestine, which are still under the colonialist yoke today?

PAUL GILROY: Thank you again for an impossible question, Ilan. I've made myself extremely unpopular by saying that all nationalisms are deeply problematic, and that governing and acting politically on the national principle will always carry ambiguities and problems with it. I follow Fanon in this, actually—at least I think I'm following him—because in those difficult gnomic sentences in *Wretched of the Earth* he identifies precisely this problem, which has occurred repeatedly.

Unfortunately I'm not familiar with Ussama Makdisi's work, but I want to say something else which connects with this sense of conviviality as having been present in the great cosmopolitan cities of the Middle East. Certainly, when I first went to Cairo many years ago this was brought home to me very strongly by the experience of looking at the city and thinking that there were similar things to be said about Baghdad, Jerusalem, and other places. Where there was a very delicate cultural ecology which was not phobic in the face of otherness, where that contact was not always felt to be contaminating.

These examples are important for me because they were all destroyed by one version of nationalism or another. That is a terribly important history to bear in mind. The other thing that happened to me was that not long after *The Black Atlantic* was published in 1993, I came across a book by Ammiel Alcalay called *After Jews and Arabs*. And my attenuated brotherhood with Ammiel Alcalay arose from the fact that we realized that we had in effect written the same book, and that we didn't know each other. We were shaped by different things. Edward [Said] was very generous in drawing attention to this overlap or intersection between the two books in his appreciative commentary on both of them. I learned a huge amount from reading Ammiel Alcalay, more than I had learned from my intermittent dialogue with Sephardim—Smadar Lavie, Ella Shohat—the people in my generation who were drawing attention to the problem that you described. But Ammiel's book, I return to—I think it's a book that merits continued study and it's not perhaps as well known as it might have been. It's not a book which is dated. In fact, the arguments that it makes about culture have an urgency about them again now.

Like June Jordan, Ammiel Alcalay is a great and thoughtful poet. He's an extraordinary poet. So maybe there's something about poets in this who are able to do things that political theorists, philosophers, and historians aren't able to do. And that poetic payoff is something that we should try to study, because it seems to me that there's something about the way that language is being used. There's something about the way in which newness is being brought into the world in this very difficult and massively overdetermined area that suggests that poets are able to summon and conjure with words in ways that are extremely important.

Now, there's something else I wanted to say about this, and it relates to the notion of "strategic essentialism." The conventional argument among leftists of my generation and older would be that nationalisms, or more wholesome varieties of nationalism which are judged to be acceptable like "nationalitarianism," create a hierarchy where some people—the dupes—need to be told that we are really all the same and interchangeable, but the elite actually understand the limitations of that. The reason I'm against the idea that nationalism can be scripted by the elite for the dupes, for the needed foot soldiers, is that hierarchy is terribly difficult to shift. Once nationalism is out and rampant and resurgent, it's not something that can be instrumentalized in a way that that political model seems to imply. So I've always been very uncomfortable, and I look to Fanon as someone who is extremely useful in drawing our attention to that, for all his profound deficiencies in some areas.

One of the things that radicalized me in the early '80s around these questions was reading in detail about the extent of nuclear cooperation that was established between the Israeli government and the South African then-apartheid regime. I think of 1948 as being the moment of apartheid, the moment of the founding of the state of Israel, and the moment of the founding of the state of Pakistan. I look at these things as being connected to one another and betraying certain fundamental tendencies in the way that politics, culture, and government are thought of in postcolonial circumstances. Now, I know that in making these comparisons or demanding an interweaving of history, I'm already trespassing into very dangerous territory.

I can remember some years ago going to hear the great political theorist and thinker Mahmood Mamdani giving the Eqbal Ahmad memorial lecture, and watching him being booed because he had dared to compare the state of Israel to the state of Liberia. I think of Faisal Devji's work on the relationship between Pakistan and Israel as political projects that share a certain affinity in the historical moment in which they appear. Of course, we face wider problems now—the way that uniqueness enters these conversations is such that any attempt to compare things is already thought by many to be an illegitimate act, an act of betrayal, or an act of treason.

We need to be stern and strong in the face of those accusations and say that, if we're going to learn more about the world and conduct ourselves better, then we have to understand how these different histories, which are already interconnected, are in relation. I make a version of this argument in thinking about the historical and empirical relationship between antisemitism and anti-Black racism over a very long period of time. 1948 is a cue or a missed opportunity to do exactly that—to see histories in relation.

It's very easy for people in conversations like this to imagine that what we think really matters, in any way. I don't know whether what we do matters and I don't think we will know. It won't be settled now; it will be something that maybe we'll find out later if we're lucky. And so, when you say that there are strong generational questions here and that you've detected amongst young Palestinians a change in perspective, a different sense of how universal and particular attachments and priorities can be thought together, this gives me a great deal of courage. Because it seems to me that we're now into a relationship with planetarity that we weren't into even very recently. How these issues will be played out in the context of the climate catastrophe, for example, or the massive displacements of people that will follow is not clear. And just as the intensity with which certain forms of national identity were held and refined and amplified, it may well be that other forms of identity, other kinds of attachments, new varieties of connectedness and association, new kinds of acting in concert will become apparent to us as these pressures grow and intensify. So I'm optimistic about that, if it's possible to be optimistic about something that's so terrifying.

What is decolonization today? My last point connects with South Africa. Given the affinities, connections, and collaborations between the apartheid South African state and the state of Israel at a certain point, my comparison wouldn't necessarily be with Liberia as with Mamdani, or with Pakistan as with Devji. I'd want to look at South Africa. The concept of apartheid may be useful in our generation because we know what apartheid was. But in conversations with younger militants and activists, it seems to me that many don't know what apartheid was in detail. We cannot assume that generational knowledge is something that we can rely on. But there are people in South Africa who have inspired me with their attempts to develop in the aftermath of that unresolved, blocked revolutionary transformation, which was so vicious, so violent, so brutal, and so incomplete. Here I think of the psychologist and sometime truth commissioner, Pumla Gobodo-Madikizela, her notion of "empathic repair" and her work with Eugene de Kock, [known as] "Prime Evil," which is a bit like [Hannah] Arendt's work with Eichmann. It's her *Eichmann in Jerusalem* account of the mentality of this man who's a murderer for the state in that context.

She's a psychologist and she's read Fanon. But she's not saying that unless we have that moment of violence that you spoke to, without that moment of national liberation, we can't proceed. She's saying that from a care with which we articulate the challenge of these difficult things in the everyday, we can find the possibility of what she calls "empathic repair." That's the horizon for me. I'm not saying it's immediately within reach, but I want to act in the immediate space and circumstances we inhabit with that horizon in mind, with that horizon as a guide for our destination.

ILAN PAPPÉ: As you talk about the horizon, both you and I, and many of the people listening to us today, are working within academia. I think it would be fitting to revisit our own profession or way of life in our final question. You already hinted about your skepticism of whether we are as crucial as sometimes we think, but nonetheless we would like to do something.

You lamented several times about certain deficiencies that appeared in academia in Britain, and maybe in general under American influence, which affected the ability to engage with the questions of racism, fascism, and the quest for a better world. One facet that you think disappeared is the willingness to take risks in discussing these issues. This is replaced by an insistence to safeguard students in "safe zones of discussion," protected by politically correct disciplinary boundaries and liberal discourses.

Now, I wonder if you have a proposed counter-pedagogy for this given the state of affairs we are in. And how does it relate to the impact of the "securitocracy," which is your term, on freedom of speech and discussion? Let me enumerate a few examples: the Prevent program; the call by the Ministry of Education for schools in Britain to teach the history of Palestine out of respect to the two narratives (that of the colonizer and the colonized, akin to asking schools at the time of apartheid to teach with respect the dogma of racial discrimination); and recently the IHRA definition that equates the reference to Zionism as racism as an act of antisemitism, when in essence it usually is an act of anticolonialism and antiracism. This is more than taking a risk that someone would boo you, be offended, or disagree with you—this can cost you your position in the system, as we know from the experiences of our colleagues.

How do we, who are part of the system, deal with this? How do you and I, for example, who are in a relatively comfortable zone, deal with these threats and deficiencies?

PAUL GILROY: How do we deal with them? Well, you ask about the IHRA definition in particular. We could start with that and I think we can do much better than that. It seems to me that the IHRA definition was not necessarily produced to deal with antisemitism on campuses—it has other functions and other aims in mind. Those who are some of its most fervent supporters have a range of objects or aims involved. So I think we can do better than that. And I say that because I'm somebody who has always believed that the practice that we must develop as antiracists, whether it's a pedagogic practice or a political one, has got to be able to show the connections between antisemitism, anti-Black racism, and other varieties of racism. That we have to be able to think these things and we have to know where racism produces racial hierarchy, where racism produces racial categories, where racism produces not just positions, but anthropologies, detail, a lexicon of racial life. It's essential.

The reason I feel so strongly about this is because I think in our country, antiracism has always been very split, politically speaking. In the sense that there are those from within Black community who generally say our focus has to be on what the government's doing—our focus has to be on the structural, the systematic, and the governmental. And there are others who say, well, actually, our focus has to be on the street and what the organized violent forces of ultranationalism, racism, and neofascism are doing.

And I've never believed that those two emphases, those two perspectives on the question of what antiracism adds up to, have to be separated from one another. I think that they are strongest, most useful, and most productive when done together. And I feel that that process can be extended. If we want to understand anti-Muslim racism, if we want to understand the production of the Muslim as a racial figure, then one of the best things we can do is look at the history of antisemitism. Because there are so many things unfolding around us right now which correspond to and connect with the things that were going on in Europe in the 1930s.

That history is a tremendous resource. Those who governmentally betray and cheapen the struggle against racism by diluting it and rearticulating it in performative denunciations are selling all of that short. That shouldn't surprise us in any way! But I think we've got enough work in our archives, we've got enough research. Yourself and other historians in Israel have taught me so very much— Idith Zertal, for example, or the things that Daniel and Jonathan

Boyarin have done. This has been tremendously enriching for me and I think the challenge is to develop arguments against the invocation of this exceptional identity in each historical setting that we find it. There are a lot of resources now that will enable us to do that. And let's look to the rising generation, even if they have a deficit of historical knowledge, and try to tap into the power of their emergent cosmopolitics. Maybe I'm wrong, but I don't think they will be stumbling over the same blocks and obstacles that we stumbled over. I think they have a different altitude at which they move.

Elias Khoury

TIMES OF STRUGGLE AND CULTURAL LIBERATION

February 17, 2022

Elias Khoury, Global Distinguished Professor at New York University from 2000 to 2014, is a public intellectual who plays a major role in the Arabic cultural scene and in the defense of the liberty of expression and democracy. He is a cultural activist who directed the theater of Beirut and codirected the Ayloul Festival of modern arts in Beirut. His academic career includes his work as a professor at Columbia University, the Lebanese University, the American University of Beirut, and the Lebanese American University. He began his career as a literary critic with his 1974 book, *Searching for a Horizon: The Arabic Novel after the Defeat of 1967* (1974). Professor Khoury then published his first novel, *On the Relations of the Circle* (1975), and became part of the Beirut vanguard in modern Arabic literature. He served on the editorial board of *Mawaqif Quarterly* and as the managing editor of *Shu'un Falastiniyya* (*Palestine Affairs*) and of *Al-Karmel Quarterly*. Professor Khoury has published fifteen novels, which have been translated into numerous languages, four books of literary criticism, and many articles and reviews. He is also known as a playwright, and his three plays have been performed in Beirut, Paris, Berlin, Vienna, and Basel. Professor Khoury has participated in writing two films and worked as a journalist, serving as director and editor-in-chief of *Mulhak*, the weekly literary supplement of *An-Nahar* newspaper in Beirut. Since 2010 he has served as the chief editor of *Majallat al-Dirasat al-Filastiniyya* (*Journal of Palestine Studies*).

ILAN PAPPÉ: Thank you for taking the time to be with us, Elias. I would like to begin with a question or two about Lebanon, your home country. The civil war in Lebanon traumatized Lebanese society as it scarred your own biography and life. It seems to be more than just an event with a closure—it appears much more as a structure, almost an unwelcome part of a nation's DNA, which you can soothe at times, but never totally cure.

Your novel *Broken Mirrors* is situated in what is allegedly known as "the postwar period," when fifteen years of civil war in Lebanon seemed to be over. As readers, we get a sense that the war trickles on and on—it does not end in your novels, regardless of whether we are able to identify the period in which they are set. It is a far more cyclic history than a linear one, which is a state of mind that characterizes the biographies of the troubled families and couples in your novels, who uneasily navigate seemingly unbridgeable relationships and yet manage to live together.

It seems for you that war and conflict in general are timeless events: they are dominated by what scholars like to call "temporality," something the Palestinians know all too well. Is what we see unfolding in Lebanon today part of this cyclic history? Or is it a new chapter, as there are no killing fields of an actual war as such—instead there is an economic and political crisis that seems to wreak disintegration and permanent uncertainty. Or is it still part of the never-ending crisis? Is there any hope for a different future for Lebanon?

ELIAS KHOURY: The question is very difficult for me because *Broken Mirrors* is a novel. And I want to point out that the civil war, which began in 1975, liberated literature in one way or another. The Lebanese literary scene was dominated by romantic nostalgic poetry and music about a unified, consolidated country that had nothing to do with the present time.

The civil war gave us—gave me and my generation—the opportunity to destroy the dominant language and to open the literary scene on what I call "writing the present." But when we write the present, the present in itself incarnates the past. And in it, there are elements of the future. You cannot write the present of a civil war, which took place in 1975, without remembering a civil war that happened in the nineteenth century, beginning in 1860. And after that war the embryo of modern Lebanon was created by the seven European powers, which were dominant at that time.

I discovered that the first civil war was never mentioned by the writers of the time or those who came later—who were great writers and the major innovators of Arabic language in the late nineteenth and early twentieth centuries. And that there was a feeling of shame in going back to an event like the civil war.

But this doesn't solve the problem! Without facing reality, without facing the present with open eyes, we cannot write. We cannot really produce literature. And the civil war provided for the emergence of the Lebanese novel—this is my theory. Before the civil war, we had novels, of course, but we didn't have a movement. Poetry was totally dominant. But with the civil war, prose and the stories of the present emerged, and the new literature was in the process of being created. Now, when I spoke about the nineteenth-century civil war, this doesn't mean we are in a cyclic situation—but also it doesn't mean we are in a linear situation. You can see this in my novels as well. Cyclic is not an accurate interpretation, nor is linear, where we are always going toward the future or the better. We are in this combination of the demons that were created in special historical circumstances and then recreated in the 1970s in another circumstance. We can speak about a kind of continuity, but there is a rupture between the civil war, as it was in the early 1970s as part of the Palestinian struggle for liberation of Palestine, and a civil war that continued after 1982, which was totally savage, as Marx said. Marx spoke about the Lebanese civil war of the nineteenth century as "the savage tribes of humans." These savage tribes came back or returned in a new form.

Civil war is not our destiny, but it is our condition now. Because a small country like Lebanon is surrounded by dictatorships. On the one hand, we have Syria and what its regime has done to the Syrian and Lebanese people. And on the other hand, we are bordered by Israel and what it recreated in the region—mainly this idea of identity based upon religion. This idea is new, it's modern. It is not an old story.

ILAN PAPPÉ: For those who may not be familiar, Western perspectives hold a view that the clash in 1860 was between Maronites and Druze communities. But I think there was also a social class issue between landowners and farmers. Looking at such a history that is not cyclic but also not linear, that has continuity but also dramatic ruptures, I'm thinking about the term "sectarianism."

We are having this conversation under the auspices of the Institute of Arab and Islamic Studies, which is of one the most important centers for Middle East studies in the UK. And "sectarianism" is one of the issues we debate academically. We feel that the term is usually employed as a classical Orientalist reductionist framing of Arab history and culture—in the context of Lebanon in particular, but also in Iraq and Syria. This framing produces a brutal political timeline and space where groups are pitted one against each other in constant conflict. And this historical view is used to provide a superficial explanation for the violence in places such as Lebanon, as well as a pretext for colonial and later imperial intervention.

Is there a better way of looking at confessional affiliations and group identities of the Mashreq's mosaic human map? Maybe as a past legacy with positive human attributes, or as a part of life (but not the whole of life) that can play a positive role today and in the future in Lebanon and beyond.

ELIAS KHOURY: I want to tell you a story that is very significant. After the French dominated Lebanon and Syria with the Sykes-Picot Agreement and the French mandate, which was typical colonialism, they tried to create five states in Syria. They created a state for the Druze in Jabal, now known as the Mount of the Druze. They created a state for the Alawites in the north and two states for the Sunnis—one in Damascus and one in Aleppo. The fifth state was called Greater Lebanon, though it was very small. The only state that survived was Lebanon—because in Lebanon there was the embryo of a confessional sectarian political structure that was built since the nineteenth century. This structure was not present in Syria. I am not saying that people did not feel affiliation to their different communities, but this affiliation was not part of their national identity. This is why the four states in Syria failed—by the will of the Syrians, not by any force. What we are witnessing now is something modern, which is related to a type of modernism of the colonial, of the political and economic structures, and of the dictatorships that came after the end of colonialism in the Arab east. What we're witnessing is the structuring of loyalties according to sect or to different confessions—and this is fabricated. When we speak about the nation, it is a fabricated issue. We invent a nation. But this does not mean that we do not have different affiliations, as I said.

This is like anywhere in the world, but here in the Arab east it is much clearer. No one has one single identity. Having one identity means you are a fascist! We have multiple layers of identities, and this is richness, not poorness. This does not automatically lead to civil wars, savagery, and massacres. This *can* lead there if a structure is pushing it forward. The Syrian dictatorship tried to dominate Syria through using one of the communities against the others, using a minority against the majority. The same thing happened in Iraq, but vice versa through the Ba'ath Party, which is a catastrophe that happened to the Arab world.

So this is invented, what we're witnessing now. And then it comes to levels of savagery with Iraq—with Da'esh [Islamic State], with what happened to the Yazidis, with what happened to the Christians of Mosul and what happened to the Christian community in Iraq under the Americans. We can go beyond this. This is something very new, it is not eternal. In our history there were factions and civil wars, but we can analyze them in a totally different way, even if it took the shape of ideology or religion. Whereas now we are witnessing something totally new, totally modern, which is threatening our national unities and our personal identities.

Once I was in France and someone introduced me as a Christian; I told them, "Please, please, please. I'm not a Christian—who told you I am Christian? I come from a Christian family, but I'm not Christian." It's not my identity. I'm Lebanese, I'm Arab. Everyone thinks I'm Palestinian and I am proud of this. This is how I figure out things and how I write—this is how I see multiple identities in my novels. There is a Muslim who was in the Jihad Muqaddas in the '30s in Palestine, whose mother is Christian. And, for him, St. Mary is part of his culture. This is how I see our identity, and this can be a great richness on one condition: to become serious about our destinies and to change this bottomless bottom that we are entering.

ILAN PAPPÉ: I'm thinking of one passage in your novel *Bab al-Shams*, or *Gate of the Sun*, that relates to this. Although it is about an individual's version of his or her own history, I think it also refers allegorically to what we are talking about. I'm thinking about where Khalil says to Yunis that he's "scared of a history that has only one version." He continues,

> History has dozens of versions, and for it to ossify into only one leads only to death. We mustn't see ourselves only in their mirror, for they're prisoners of one story, as though that story had abbreviated and ossified them. . . . You mustn't become just one story. . . . I see you as a man who betrays and repents and loves and fears and dies. This is the only way if we're not to ossify and die.

This relates to his personal life, of course. But I think it is also a kind of philosophy and your reaction to a reductionist politics of identity, which is not a continuation of the mosaic of the past. It is a modern creation and a deadly one.

Let me move to Palestine here. Since you were nineteen years old, you have been deeply involved in the Palestinian liberation movement and Palestinian cultural life. There are currently many efforts and initiatives to either reformulate, repeal, or replace the fragmentation caused by the Nakba and subsequent events that created different Palestinian constituencies with different agendas.

And it seems that the younger Palestinian generation is looking for a way forward to be guided out of the present deadlock, hopefully by new democratic and representative leadership. Are you involved in these kinds of contemplations? And even if you are not, what are your views on the future political structure that may have the ability to carry the Palestinian liberation struggle forward in this century?

ELIAS KHOURY: I was and I think I still am a militant, but I was never a political politician. So don't expect a political answer from me in the narrow concept of "politics." Since you referred to Yunis and *Bab al-Shams,* I want to remind you that after the defeat of 1967, there's a scene where Yunis is in the camp and he says to everyone, "From the beginning, we have to begin again." I think we are now in a moment which is very similar to that moment. We need a new beginning. This is what is vibrating in my eyes, and in my soul. This is what I felt when Bassel al-Araj was assassinated by the Israelis.[1]

This is what I felt last week when three youngsters from Nablus were assassinated. This is what I felt when the six prisoners escaped Gilboa Prison through a tunnel. We need a new beginning. I don't believe that we can revive something that died. Revival can only be done by gods and we are not gods. We are human beings. In history there is no revival. In history, there are beginnings, and the beginning must be from the base—from the struggle and resistance against the occupation, apartheid, and the closed national identitarian discourse. The struggle for a free and democratic Palestine, where Palestinians have the right to return, where we can hope for a future for the children, grandchildren, and great-grandchildren of the refugees who have been through hell for seventy-four years.

So we need a new beginning. In this beginning I try to be part of the debate. And we are old now—we are no longer "fit" for the technical struggle, which I did when I was young. But I think struggle has many forms, and one of its forms is writing and literature. I think Palestine now is literature.

In the artistic pluralistic perspective, Palestine has a special place—I say this not only because I love the Palestinians. Here, you have a situation where there is colonization, there is apartheid, and there are colonies (referred to as "settlements" in a technical error). I do not have any hope in the leadership that dominates the PLO. I do not have any hope in Hamas that is using Gaza. I think we need something totally new.

We need something totally new in a new situation where the Arab dictatorships have shown us their real face—that they are another face of colonialism and Zionism. The Palestinians are not alone. They are alone if they separate their struggle from the struggle of the Arabs for democracy and from the struggle for equality and humanity on the international level. We are not alone. But we need to find ways to rebuild this collective struggle and feeling around Palestine.

ILAN PAPPÉ: When you say that we should start from the beginning, I was thinking about your longtime engagement with the events of the Nakba as a writer, as a novelist. And later you added another layer, having a dialectical relationship between the Nakba and the Holocaust in your novels—between Jewish history or the history of persecution of the Jews and the history of the Zionist colonization and oppression of the Palestinians.

I'd like to ask you about this engagement with the Nakba and its denial. One of the features of dealing with the Nakba is the way you and many others would refer to the Nakba as *al-Nakba al-mustamirrah*—the ongoing Nakba. There's a certain sense of desperation because it seems that the most common references to the Nakba are its persistence and constant denial. Your novels bring it back, as did the poems of Mahmoud Darwish, as did the work of the historians—just recently we were able to resurface the crime of the massacre that occurred in Tantura in 1948. It is a denial that is forced by the oppressor, but also brought by the victims' inability and unwillingness to speak, as we learn from Adam Danun's notebooks in *Children of the Ghetto*.

How much should this struggle against denial be part of the liberation struggle you are talking about? You highlighted the role that literature should play and I agree with you! How much of it is also a struggle against denial of the Nakba? And to what extent is a struggle against denial part of decolonization—part of the struggle for liberation and not an unhealthy nostalgic adherence to the past?

Is it part of what Edward Said used to call a demand for "permission to narrate," or is it much more than that? Is it exactly what you talked about: the right of return? Is it not a demand to fight against denial because we want not only acknowledgment of the crime of the Nakba, we also want accountability for the crimes committed by Israel—and we believe they are best rectified through the right of return. Is this something that we should continue to focus on?

And if I can add, how do you see the dialectical connection between the Nakba and the Holocaust? Your involvement is an antidote to what we are experiencing in Britain due to the new IHRA definition, where criticism of Israel can now be framed as denial of the Holocaust. It stifles debate and our ability to pursue constructive criticism.

I would like you to talk about the Nakba and its connection to the Holocaust through the quote from Adam Danun, who says in *Children of the Ghetto*, "I did not conceal my Palestinian identity, but I hid it in the Palestinian ghetto [in al-Lid, Lod] in which I was born. I was a son of the ghetto and it bestowed upon me the immunity of the Warsaw Ghetto." To those who are not familiar with the term "ghetto" in this context, let me explain that the Palestinians who remained in the destroyed towns of Palestine after the Nakba were cordoned in areas and circled with barbed wire, which the Israelis themselves called "the ghetto."

What you are doing, if I understood correctly, is providing immunity through a certain mode of resistance in the past that persecuted Jews were using, and shielding yourself by almost appropriating the term "ghetto," which the Israelis invoked. And you create an interesting relationship as part of a literary attempt—and not a political attempt—to explain the importance of not denying the Nakba, of commemorating it and examining its relevance for the present.

ELIAS KHOURY: I first used the term "the ongoing Nakba" in a lecture I gave at the annual lecture for the Wissenschaftskolleg Institute for Advanced Studies in Berlin. I don't know why they chose me, but the hall was full of German professors and German heads of universities. It was very prestigious. And I read a long text, which was republished afterward in English and Arabic. To my astonishment, the reaction was . . . first of all, nobody clapped for ten seconds. And then everybody did.

But the reaction and real anger was, "You are speaking about the Nakba now and the Nakba happened in '48—*khalas!*" There was no denying of the Nakba. They couldn't deny it. But they wanted to deny that what we are living through now is the Nakba, that this is the Nakba taking different forms. This is what makes it different from the Holocaust—I do not say the Holocaust and the Nakba are the same thing. One of the differences is that the Holocaust happened. The Nakba *is* happening. This is the present of Palestine and this is the present of the Arabs. It's happening now—in Sheikh Jarrah, in Nablus, everywhere in Palestine and historic Palestine. In all of Palestine in '48 and '67, in all of Gaza the Nakba is happening. What we are witnessing is the same project, which is continuing. When [historian] Benny Morris republished his book after the second intifada, he said that Ben-Gurion committed a big error when he did not continue. The first declaration by Ariel Sharon at the beginning of the second intifada was, "We are in a new war of independence," which means we are in the Nakba. The war of independence is not finished. There is a continuous process which is still taking place and our struggle is to stop this process. The moment we stop this process, everything will change.

In this sense, the Nakba is not a memory. It is the present, and memory comes from the present. You mentioned the ghetto of Lydda—there were many ghettos: Lydda, Ramle, Haifa, Jaffa. The Palestinians in the ghetto heard the term for the first time from Israeli soldiers. And to my astonishment many people told me, "Isn't it the name of the Arab quarter, of the Arab neighborhood?" They thought this is the name Israel gave to the Arab neighborhood—"ghetto."

It was not by accident that the Israeli soldiers called them ghettos—in their subconscious they knew what they were doing. We are revisiting Tantura and just witnessing it with the film (*Tantura*, 2022). I think these criminals were aware of their criminality. There is a beautiful Israeli novel, *Khirbet Khizeh* by S. Yizhar. S. Yizhar was a Zionist, but I taught his novel. And for those doing comparative literature, it's interesting to compare *Khirbet Khizeh* to Palestinian literature.

The novel was published in 1949, during the war of the Nakba, during the war of independence. Yizhar describes the Palestinians who are expelled from this village—he called it "Khirbet Khizeh," but we later learned it was the actual village Khirbet al-Khisas—as if they are Jews. He uses the same terms that the antisemites use to describe the Jews, which makes them "the Jews of the Jews."

The Nakba and the Holocaust are related through this concept, the Jews and "the Jews of the Jews." And it seems all societies and all types of racism need Jews, as a figure. If you don't have Jews, you invent your Jews! The same thing is taking place now in Europe: they are inventing their Jews from the Muslims. So practically it is no longer possible to understand the Holocaust without understanding the Nakba, or to understand the Nakba without understanding the Holocaust.

This doesn't mean that one crime and another crime make us equal. The Holocaust is a crime that we must condemn, and the Nakba is a crime that we must condemn. But the Nakba is still taking place and we must be accountable. Otherwise, we cannot escape this vicious circle. I know this will not sound realistic, but I am not realistic.

You need a dream. You need a dream to write books. You need a dream to make a revolution. You need a dream to teach deep from your heart. Otherwise, it's meaningless.

This relationship between the Nakba and the Holocaust will open a horizon for reconciliation. Not in the way that the Oslo agreements framed reconciliation, because it was a surrender, which the Israelis refused. We need a deep reconciliation of accepting the other and trying to build a new democratic place—a place where our religious identity is not the dominant identity. The dominant identity is our human identity. This is how I dream.

And I think this is what gave me the potential to write a novel like *Children of the Ghetto*. This dream enabled me to go through this very dark history, which is as if you are going inside your dark selves—this is the heart of darkness. This is the real heart of darkness that literature can help us to understand. Not to solve, but to understand. How to solve it is up to the new generation, who must teach us.

ILAN PAPPÉ: I have a final question for you, Elias. At the beginning of our conversation, you said the civil war, in a way, liberated a certain generation of Lebanese writers, and you connected to past and present events. That reminded me of Isabel Allende once saying that, unlike in the West, audiences in Latin America anticipate their writers to have a certain message—ideological, moral, political. She had the sense that even with a romance story, the audience anticipates a reference to political, ideological, and moral issues.

When you look toward the next generation of writers in the Arab world, do you think there is a sense that writing or the novel, with all its multilayered objectives, is part of the liberation struggle? You once said that you want to make people feel the joy of the novel, to make people happy, interested, or moved. But there is also the wish not to solve or offer a solution, but to illuminate a question, to expand on it. Do you feel that the current generation of writers on Palestine or Lebanon see themselves as part of liberation, fighting against injustice? Or is there more an escape, to say "this is so horrible or insoluble that we don't want to be there"? Can you provide a final statement of the role of literature in a part of the world that needs decolonization, especially de-Zionization, and a better record of human and civil rights?

ELIAS KHOURY: When we were speaking about translation, we said that translators must be poets and they must not consider the audience at all. When I write, I don't think about the audience. I think about what I am trying to discover, what I am trying to go through, what I am trying to experience. Because every novel is like a journey. Every novel presents something to learn about, discover, and *then* to come back and to read. In *One Thousand and One Nights*, Sinbad used to travel to far places actually in order to tell—because he was a storyteller. So he came back to tell. I go in order to tell, and I tell what I've seen. I don't tell what I think is good.

To go back to *Bab al-Shams*, the plan was to write a love story—I swear it was. The initial plan had nothing to do with Palestine. The initial plan was that Yunis is living in Lebanon, he has a wife who is in the Galilee, and he wants to cross the border. To go and meet, because he was in love her. And I said to myself, "This is the first story." Because normally the story of love in literature is the story of separation. And you never love your wife! You love someone else. Here I thought we are going toward a new approach about love. And then when I put Yunis in his context, all of Palestine, I was obliged. Instead of writing a novel in one year—a small, short novel about love—I spent seven, eight years in order to build the whole story. But the whole story was around love.

So you discover and you witness what you are discovering. I think this is what literature is all about. And now reading it in the situation I am and the situation the text is, of course this is part of decolonization—because I am part of decolonization. But I do not push the text to follow me. I follow the text. I do not teach the heroes what to say, they teach me how to speak.

It's a very complex relationship, but practically my heroes are marginals. This is a choice, because I feel I'm a margin. Strangers, because I feel I am a stranger. The way Adam Danun is, or the way Khalil Ayub is. This is how I feel. This is who I identify with. I think that now in the Mashreq we are witnessing something. For example, there is a huge innovation with the Syrian novel that has happened over twelve years, since the beginning of the so-called Arab Spring. It's amazing how the Syrian novel became so central in Syrian culture! How the Iraqi novel traveled the same road that the Lebanese novel took fifty years ago.

I'm a reader and I learn from these young, new writers. I do not teach them. When I read them, I'm so happy! Now, many of them feel that it's too much, that you have to go aside. I think you cannot.

Wherever you are, we are witnessing. At the beginning you asked me personally about Beirut. This is the first time in my life I feel that I am in exile when I'm in Beirut.

The exile became an interior part of our lives, whether we are in Beirut, or in Baghdad, or in Damascus, or in Paris, or in London, or in Berlin. Wherever we are, we are in exile. And I think this experience of the literature, of exile, will give something new. I don't know what. But there is something profoundly new, which is beginning. I'm very enthusiastic to read because practically, who is the writer? The writer is the reader. You read the reality and you translate it. When you read a novel or a poem, when I go back to my great friend and personal poet Mahmoud Darwish, I feel as if I am taking all the languages. Not only Arabic! I'm taking all the languages.

In one language, you feel all the languages. You feel the ancient languages, which were dominant in our part of the world—especially the Aramaic, the Syriac, the Hebrew, and so on. And you take the modern languages. In one poem, you can incarnate the whole world. In one novel, the whole world will come, and you'll be part of it.

Gabor Maté

ON TRAUMA AND
(THE LIMITS OF) COMPASSION

March 17, 2022

Gabor Maté is a retired physician who, after twenty years of family practice and palliative care experience, worked for over a decade in Vancouver's Downtown Eastside with patients challenged by drug addiction and mental illness. The best-selling author of five books published in forty languages, Gabor is an internationally renowned speaker highly sought after for his expertise on addiction, trauma, childhood development, and the relationship between stress and illness. His book on addiction received the Hubert Evans Prize for literary nonfiction. For his groundbreaking medical work and writing, he has been awarded the Order of Canada, his country's highest civilian distinction, and the Civic Merit Award from his hometown, Vancouver. His books include: *In the Realm of Hungry Ghosts: Close Encounters with Addiction* (2018); *When the Body Says No: The Cost of Hidden Stress* (2019); *Scattered*

Minds: The Origins and Healing of Attention Deficit Disorder (2019); and *Hold on to Your Kids: Why Parents Need to Matter More than Peers* (2019, with Gordon Neufeld). Gabor's most recent book, *The Myth of Normal: Trauma, Illness, and Healing in a Toxic Culture*, was published in 2022.

ILAN PAPPÉ: When we start such a conversation in this particular moment, we cannot avoid mentioning Ukraine, even if our series focuses on decolonization in Palestine. We feel compassion toward the victims of the brutal war waged on that country, and anger at those who have the ability to stop the war and do not. And yet, Western media and political coverage of the war has exposed high levels of hypocrisy—particularly if you are aware of the human-made and nature-made catastrophes in the Arab world, the African continent, the inner cities of North America, the pueblos of South America, and in Palestine.

I would like to speak with you about this by attempting to associate your world of treating, healing, and caring for the individual's mental and medical health with my world of recording the chronicles of groups of people, nations, and minorities, who are individually and collectively under daily oppression and whose only crime is their perceived identity and location. I will preface our conversation with the following question: How far can we go in projecting or applying your insights on trauma, fear, depression, and addiction, which are interconnected in the treatment of the individual, to an analysis of collectives—be they nations, movements, minorities, or groups bound by a shared identity?

Can we talk about a collective trauma? Can we talk about addictions to ideologies, to fanaticism, to warmongering, to self-victimization, or to the victimization of others by using the same methodology, in order to learn why traumas are invisible? How can we make them visible, and what impact do they have on our lives when they are denied?

Let's unpack one example: ideology. Can ideology be defined as an addiction? Can a harmful ideology be sustained either because of denial of its harm, or because it seems to be pursued as a passion but, in fact, it is both self-harmful and harmful to others? Intuitively, as a historian I feel that this could be an extremely helpful dimension, which I haven't explored, or a new entry point to chronicling inhumanity as a major topic—especially in Palestine, but not only there. And being moved to tears when discovering the rays of humanity there.

As a personal inclination, I am not sure whether this has become an addiction in a way. Preparing for this talk, I remember that Edward Said once called me a "Nakba junkie." Fondly, I should say! I still believe it is a passion to know, or to want to know, what happened in 1948 during the Nakba—as a pursuit of justice and not addiction to inhumanities or massacres. But I feel this is much more ambiguous after reading your work.

Racism, fanaticism, and the harmful dehumanization of others are at the heart of the chronicles of inhumanity that I narrate. Can we relate them to the realm of your compassionate approach to people who are addicted, in the broadest possible meaning of the term?

GABOR MATÉ: You are asking me a multilayered question, and I'm not sure that I am adequate to respond to it. But let me begin. First, you touched upon Ukraine. It is both quite astonishing and dismaying to see what's happening right now. We agree on the unjustifiability of the war, the cruelty of it.

But it is the hypocrisy that strikes me the most. Three weeks ago, a *New York Times* columnist published an article with the headline "'This Is True Barbarity': Life and Death under Russian

Occupation." We've just woken up again, as if we thought barbarism is over. I wanted to respond, "Have you heard about Iraq? Have you heard about Yemen? Have you heard about Guatemala? Have you heard about Gaza? Have you heard about the Occupied Territories? You are just waking up to the reality that there's barbarism in the world? What kind of selective mindset would ignore all that?"

Here in Vancouver, a young Russian pianist was invited to play at a musical concert organization—he is now being banned. And the tennis association is talking about banning the Russian players, like Medvedev and Rublev, from tournaments. I think that's great—let's sanction the Russians. But let's also exclude any Canadian athletes because Canada sells weapons to the Saudis, which they use to murder Yemenis. Let's also sanction the Americans for any number of internationally known killings, massacres, and invasions, which are much larger when compared with Ukraine. Let's also sanction the UK. The UK has no right to be in any sports tournaments given its history and its current engagements.

The hypocrisy comes out of ideology. By its very nature, an ideology includes and it excludes. And it has hidden blind spots, which preclude it from allowing any material that would challenge it to penetrate.

I have my own particular history—let me talk about my serial disillusionment. I grew up in communist Hungary, a Jewish infant survivor of the genocide. The Soviet army were my heroes, they saved my life. I also believed in the system. And then there was the '56 revolution against this brutal Stalinist oppression that I wasn't aware of as a child because my parents weren't telling me about it. So I got disillusioned. Then we came to the West and that was America, the shining city on the hill. Four years later, they're massacring millions of Vietnamese on television, supported by the press. So I got disillusioned there. And then I was a Zionist and I got disillusioned with *that*. I'm talking about the value of disillusion, by the way. It's good to be disillusioned. I would always ask people, "Would you rather be illusioned or disillusioned? Would you rather know the truth, or would you rather hold on to fancy ideas?"

As a young Zionist leader, I was given the task of giving a talk on how to counter Arab propaganda on university campuses. I thought, "Well, if I'm going to counter Arab propaganda on campuses, maybe I should find out what Arab propaganda actually says." That's when I started looking into the other side. When I say the other side, I didn't read Arab propaganda—I read Jewish sources about Zionism, long before Ilan and his fellow new historians came on the scene. But there was already enough evidence in '67 to lead me to conclude that what happened was the exclusion of one people to establish a land for another. That what happened in '67 was a very deliberately concocted war, which Ilan has eloquently documented. So I then present my point of view, not yet believing in it, and my fellow Zionists were angry with me. "How can you be saying these things?" And I said, "I'm just pretending to be an Arab speaking my side." I fulfilled the assignment, but they were upset with me for doing too good a job of it. So, one more disillusionment.

An ideology is addictive, in a certain sense. Let me define addiction for you. An addiction is manifested in any behavior that a person finds relief or pleasure in and therefore craves and holds on to despite negative consequences—they do not give it up despite those negative consequences. I don't want to call ideology *exactly* an addiction, but it has features in common.

It does provide psychological comfort to people. When you're a Zionist, you have a reason to live, you have meaning, you have a collective, you have a history that makes sense to you. You get to be both a victim but also a victor, which is deeply satisfying. In other words, you don't need to deal with your vulnerability. All addiction is about not dealing with vulnerability. Addiction is about being so hurt and vulnerability threatens you so much, you try to numb yourself to your vulnerability.

As an ideology, Zionism is an antidote to vulnerability. Because now we have an answer to everything and we can justify whatever we do. We don't need to be vulnerable. We don't need to look at the truth. Ideologies are very seductive and they work. Like the addict is in denial of the problem that he is creating for himself, let alone for other people, a person who is attracted or addicted to an ideology will be in denial of the harm being done to themselves and particularly to others.

So, yes, I think it's useful to talk about ideology as addictive. Just as addiction, in my view, is people's attempt not to feel their pain. It's understandable. In the same way, when I think of my grandparents who were killed in Auschwitz, that's very painful. If I can believe that there's redemption, response, and revenge through a particular state and its activities, then I can then deal with or not feel as much the pain of what happened.

Ideologies and addictions have a lot in common—mostly the rigid incapacity and unwillingness to look at the truth of it.

ILAN PAPPÉ: Let's talk a bit more about disillusionment, denial, and how we confront them in the situations we face in Canada and Israel, looking toward past evils and in current evils. We both come from a European Jewish background, with different trajectories and different fields of professional interest. And yet, in many ways, our concern about Palestine and the Palestinians is our first meeting point. But I noticed in an interview you gave to *Haaretz*, at the end of the interview (which is typical to Israeli journalists) they asked you about your take on Israel and Palestine—as if this were a passing issue and not entirely related to the conversation on crime, addiction, and trauma. I would like to take a different approach. I would rather have a general discussion about these issues as related to Palestine and other concerns including decolonization, racism, and social justice.

To fuse what you did in Canada and what is unfolding in Palestine, which we are both watching with horror, let us talk about our two settler-colonial societies. Two political projects established in the past with the help of what the late Patrick Wolfe called "the logic of the elimination of the native." These settler-colonial societies, Canada and Israel, still by and large deny their past—and this denial enables them to continue the elimination in the present.

But we both approach it with some caution, I think. You express your sense of gratitude for a Canada that received you and your family, which is probably akin to what I should have felt toward Zionism in Palestine, which gave refuge to my parents escaping from Nazi Germany in the 1930s. We both were unaware of the settler-colonial setting, genocide, and ethnic cleansing that accompanied these two safe havens for our families, and probably our lives changed when we learned of these atrocities.

You dealt with it in a very positive way when you told the *Toronto Star*, "For Canadians to be truly strong and free, we must come to terms with our grim past"—a quote which leads me to assert that these are not just personal journeys we have taken. We were and are guided by the Indigenous victims of these colonization projects who helped us to decolonize our knowledge. Without this struggle for liberation, we have no way of changing the ideological systems that have power to continue narrating their version of history, as well as continuing the colonization that this narrative is meant to justify.

We can treat Canadian and Israeli denial as a political situation. But from what you are saying, it seems that this is also a mental situation. Can we also treat that denial in the way you would treat denial when you meet patients or clients who deny their trauma, depression, and addiction? I have some frustration when applying this process to Israel. As an activist I do believe that some measure of acknowledgment and even co-resistance must come from the settler or colonialist community for the healing process, namely decolonization, to succeed. But to begin this, you need to be able to elicit some compassion from the Israeli Jews for the Palestinian plight, and this hardly exists.

Do you feel that a similar problem prevents such a process in Canada? As you are leading the way in showing compassion to addicts in a society that tends to view them as criminals rather than victims, perhaps your interaction with the state antidrug policy and the overall culture of social denial and criminalization can help us. Not least to deal with the lack of compassion in our societies, which I feel is the main hurdle to starting a conversation about denial. Because as long as Israel would be in a state of denial, in the double meaning of "a state of denial," I can see no way of ending the violence that Israel imposes on the Palestinians, wherever they are.

GABOR MATÉ: Canada did receive our family with open arms, and we appreciated it. I didn't know what was happening here. The same year that we arrived in British Columbia as Hungarian refugees, in 1957, there was a native woman who was then four years old. I've met her since and her name is Carlene. She was taken to a residential school, which were places run by the churches where the government mandated that native children be abducted from their families. They were not permitted to see their parents, who were threatened with jail if they tried to see their kids. In these residential schools, children were abused emotionally, sexually, physically, culturally, spiritually, and starved as well. Thousands died. This last summer, June of 2021, they discovered a group of bodies of young children. This wasn't news to the Indigenous population—they had been talking about these missing children for decades. But here was proof. Thousands of bodies were discovered. Two weeks before these bodies were discovered, a public opinion poll found that 70 percent of Canadians said they knew nothing or little about the residential schools. In a certain sense, this is astonishing. In another sense, it's an artifact of colonialism and denialism.

Now, in that same year that I arrived in Canada, Carlene was taken to a residential school. She made the mistake of speaking her own language, her tribal language. The punishment was that she had a pin stuck in her tongue—and for a whole hour this little girl couldn't put her tongue back in her mouth because she would cut her lips. That's before the sexual abuse began. She was an alcoholic by the time she was nine years old. Can you imagine? And her grandchildren are now drug addicted. Two weeks after these bodies were discovered, a prominent Canadian pseudo-journalist named Conrad Black, who was knighted by the queen, wrote an article saying, "What's the big deal about a few dead bodies?"

It's illegal to deny the Holocaust in Canada, but it's perfectly legal to deny the cultural and physical genocide of native people. That's denial. And the denial has two bases. First, if you're the perpetrator and you want to continue to perpetrate, then you just need to deny that you're perpetrating. But that's not where most people come from in their denial. For most people, the source of denial is a confluence of personal history and large-scale, societal history.

Denial happens when to admit the facts is just too painful. A lot of people are traumatized in this culture, more than we realize. For them to be aware of how they were hurt by people who love them or were meant to love them is too painful to admit, so they're in denial. What I'm saying is that in this culture, regardless of the history or perpetration of genocide, people are individually, on a large scale, psychologically programmed to be in denial about the reality of the world.

When people are psychologically minded to deny, that will then support large-scale historical denial. Furthermore, there's a kind of passivity that this society engenders in people. Who really wants the Earth to be destroyed? But what are most people doing about it? Nothing. The psychologist Erich Fromm talked about "social character." The social character is inculcated to the family of origin, but it serves the social purpose of making people fit into the society as it is structured. So apart from the personal denial that feeds the social denial, there's also this passivity. If you ask the average Israeli, Canadian, or British person, "Put together three intelligent sentences about the history of Palestine," they couldn't do it. You can ask the average British person, whose country participated in the invasion of Iraq with the death of over half a million people, "Put together three intelligent sentences on the history of Iraq or of Afghanistan." Or right now, "Give me three intelligent sentences about the history of Ukraine in the last ten years." They couldn't do it. Because an ingrained passivity is built into the social character, and that serves the interest of the social-political structure that it is designed to perpetuate. Because people are in denial and people are passive. So here's where the personal psychological feeds into the social and historical.

ILAN PAPPÉ: I recognize it so easily when thinking about Israel. Just recently, an Israeli filmmaker was able to expose the mass graves of a horrific massacre that happened in 1948, which was denied for many years.[1] This documentary film provided the most important solid evidence for what we have been claiming happened. He told me that now the whole discussion about the atrocities committed in 1948 will change in Israel.

I said to him, "It won't change. Because even the people you are interviewing, who admit perpetrating the massacre, say, 'Hey, why do you want to talk about it? There's no need.' And secondly, they lived for many years denying that massacre, which reflects the society's denial of that event." So the connection between the individual denial of one's own part and accountability and the overall orchestrated denial by the state go hand in hand.

But when you talk about the First Nations in Canada and the Indigenous community, I also notice that you not only tell us the horrific experiences that they had, but you also feel that we have a lot to learn from them, as I do when I talk to Palestinians. Both in your medical treatment and your overall comprehension of reality. In this respect, in Canada we can see how decolonization is connected with Indigenous rights but also, and because of that, with ecology.

You had a dialogue with a group called Indigenous Climate Action (ICA) that works on the assumption that ecological disasters and disruptions are an ongoing traumatic event, or even a structure, that spans generations. Eriel Tchekwie Deranger, the founder and director of ICA, said that the trauma of climate change in Canada—but not only in Canada—"is interwoven into colonization in the form of modern extraction practices." So colonization is based on denying the intricate, maybe even organic, relations between identity and our natural surroundings. You told this group, "If we somehow learned how to drop our arrogance, and I mean the arrogance of Western/Northern culture, and opened ourselves to learning, what could we learn from you and bring us back to ourselves and stop this madness?"

This unlearning and learning can help us to decolonize our ecological world. Where are we with this dialogue in Canada, in not only telling the chronicles of what has been done, but respecting Indigenous communities as a group that can teach us how to deal with ecology, nature, and reality?

GABOR MATÉ: There's a lot to be learned. Let me tell you a story. In my field of medicine—there are terrific achievements in Western medicine, but it's also hopelessly narrow in its perspective. It separates entities that in real life are inseparable. It separates the mind from the body.

When you go see the average physician with a chronic medical problem, they're never going to ask you about your childhood, your traumas, your personal relationships, how you feel about yourself as a human being, your stresses on the job. And yet, these have everything to do with why most people get sick, chronically. They separate the mind from the body. They separate the individual from the environment, so that disease is seen as a biological event in an organ.

Now, that's not how it works in reality. I'll give you a couple of examples. The more racism a Black American woman experiences, the greater her risk for asthma. Indigenous women in Canada, who never used to have any rheumatoid arthritis or autoimmune disease prior to colonization, now have six times the rate of rheumatoid arthritis of any other person in Canada. I won't go into the reasons, but it is related to suppression and self-repression, which is imposed by a colonialist, male-dominated society. The patriarchy.

But Western medicine doesn't make those connections, despite all kinds of evidence. It's not that we don't have the science—we have the science! We just choose not to look at it. Talk about an ideological blinder. By contrast, I was talking to a colleague of mine, an American physician and psychiatrist who is part Lakota Sioux. He said that in the Lakota tradition, when someone gets sick, the whole community gathers and says, "Thank you. Your illness is manifesting the pathology of the whole community. And so your healing is our healing."

From the perspective of hard science, that's much more scientifically accurate than the split Western view. And that's not the only area in which we could learn a lot. We could learn about resilience. Dire and horrific as the situation is in some of Canada's First Nations communities with the impacts of multigenerational abuse, and dire and horrific as the situation often is in Palestine, I'm sure that you have been as impressed as I have with the sheer resilience of people. With their capacity to survive, endure, and continue to create and have positive responses, even in the face of unbearable oppression.

I know a woman in Jericho who does Sufi dancing in her work with Palestinian children who have spent months in jail without being allowed to see their parents. Her neck was broken by the Israeli army, and an Israeli surgeon saved her, but she dances with these children. How do you have that kind of positive energy after your neck has been broken and when you are so oppressed? We can learn a lot about resilience.

We can learn a lot about the unity of all beings. When an Indigenous person thinks of a river, the river is part of them and they are part of the river. That's a totally different way of relating. You aren't looking at an object "out there"—they are looking at an entity that is a part of them. It's hard to put it into words, but this is a point of view that could save us and the planet, if we learned.

ILAN PAPPÉ: I want to take it a bit further in thinking about the way that we are dealing with the COVID-19 crisis, especially in Western societies. You've given us a warning about the risks of basing medicine on biology and chemistry alone, and cautioned against the conventional rejection of a more holistic approach to illness and treatment. As you put it, the norm is treating disease as an independent entity—an approach that decontextualizes illnesses from its social, cultural, and even political environments.

Was this approach also the basis of how Western societies, governments, and even the World Health Organization (WHO) dealt with COVID-19 and still are dealing with it? Can there be another approach to the pandemic?

GABOR MATÉ: I think it will take time for us to really absorb the lessons of the Covid experience, but some things are already apparent. Who is more prone to getting Covid? In Britain, it was Black people, Asian people—people of color. They were more likely to get Covid or to die from it. That's not an isolated biological fact. That's a social fact of who is oppressed, who has power, and who is stressed.

Boris Johnson, the former prime minister, was hospitalized. He spent time in an ICU, came out, and became a weight-loss evangelist. Because he says that obesity is a risk factor for Covid. But what causes obesity? The last few decades have seen an epidemic of obesity in the West, and throughout the world, with the spread of neoliberalism. The obesity epidemic is not separate from the oppression and stress that people experience when economic and social conditions become more challenging. But Johnson would never talk about *that* in his anti-obesity campaign.

Furthermore, if we understood the world from a genuinely global sense and knowing that viruses know no geographical or political boundaries, we wouldn't have given the vaccine to all the healthy people in the rich countries. We would have inoculated the vulnerable people all over the world. That would have been a far more effective public health measure.

But of course, it's "we have the money, we have the power." Not to mention that governments gave enormous sums of money to private companies to develop the vaccine, yet they share none of the profits. Some of these companies are making $1,000 per second from a product that was developed with government money. So not Covid, not anything, can be separated from the global colonial situation.

If we didn't have a colonial mentality, if we saw someone in South Africa or India or Papua New Guinea or Latin America as important as we are and as valid members of the community that we're a part of, then we would not make decisions based on privilege. We would make decisions based on inclusion. And that certainly hasn't happened in this Covid crisis. Not to mention the outrageous amounts of money that the pharmaceutical companies want to charge poorer countries. Why don't they just make the patent available to everyone? Are we humanitarians or are we profiteers? Well, we're profiteers, which is the essence of colonialism. In Israel, they inoculated all the Israelis, but the Palestinians? "That's not our responsibility. Let them do it themselves."

ILAN PAPPÉ: I think one of the problems is that there is an intricate explanation here. Above every other problem we have in challenging the narrative given to justify these unjust policies, we don't always have the time span or the ability to elicit the patience of people to hear and listen to a more intricate explanation. You cannot do these things by sound bites. You really need a space for it.

A final question for the activists among us. One of the really impressive things in your biography is your willingness to risk lawlessness, and maybe even prison, when you refuse to adhere to policies or instructions that prohibit the administration of drugs to addicts. You do this so that people will not resort to a lethal overdose in case of an abrupt withdrawal or detoxification process, and when using traditional or Indigenous medicine in your clinic.

Many of our students are also activists and they keep asking themselves how far they can take their action and activism vis-à-vis the law of the land, the regulation. Do you have a sense of when it's time to break the law in a seemingly democratic society? How far we can go with this? Because you must have consciously known that you were disobeying a policy, regulation, or even a law in some of your actions in Vancouver.

Is this part of social activism and our role in the struggle against denial and oppression? Is it part of learning from the resilience of those on the receiving end of these colonialist and racist practices?

GABOR MATÉ: It would be an over-valorization of my own history to say that I've ever really faced any serious threat to my liberty. I was never in that kind of situation. I don't know what I would have done if I had been. I'd like to think I would have acted on principle, but who really knows? You don't know until you're up against it.

What I faced, personally, is when in 1967 I wrote an article that Israel started this war to take over the territories. I was kicked out of my father's house. To give him credit, he came around later in life and started to see reality. So first you face a decision to make. Do you want to speak your truth, or do you want to maintain your emotional relationships if the truth threatens those relationships? I think that's an important question for all of us. I can't tell anyone else what to do, but I've never been able to stay silent about things that I felt were important to speak about, including Israel/Palestine. And that's cost me some relationships, but that's the price you pay.

I'm in no position to advise anyone about breaking the law or not. There are many inspiring examples here in Canada right now. Young people are protesting against the further takeover and destruction of native resources. They're being treated brutally by the police, and the press doesn't even report it. Police brutality is not news in this country. But I haven't done that myself. A friend of mine—a seventy-six-year-old grandmother who stands up to my eyebrows—was arrested for threatening the peace because she stood on the bridge blocking traffic as a protest against the destruction of native lands.

I can't advise anyone because I don't know what I would do if I were confronted with that kind of a choice. I think the question we need to keep asking ourselves is: What is the truth worth to us and what are we willing to give up in order to serve the truth, as we understand it? That's a highly individual question. Throughout history some people have given—and continue to give—brave answers to that question.

Nadera Shalhoub-Kevorkian

ON LIFE AND DEATH IN PALESTINE

September 21, 2022

Nadera Shalhoub-Kevorkian is the Lawrence D. Biele Chair in Law at the Faculty of Law-Institute of Criminology and the School of Social Work and Public Welfare at the Hebrew University of Jerusalem. She is also the Global Chair in Law at Queen Mary University of London. Her research focuses on trauma, state crimes and criminology, surveillance, gender violence, law, and society. She studies the crime of femicide and other forms of gender-based violence, violence against children in conflict areas, crimes of abuse of power in settler-colonial contexts, surveillance, securitization, and social control. Her published books include: *Militarization and Violence against Women in Conflict Zones in the Middle East: A Palestinian Case-Study* (2010); *Security Theology, Surveillance and the Politics of Fear* (2015); *Incarcerated Childhood and the Politics of Unchilding* (2019); and the edited books *Understanding Campus-Community Partnerships in Conflict Zones* (2019), *When Politics Are Sacralized* (2021), and *The Cunning of Gender*

Violence (2023). *Incarcerated Childhood* won the 2020 Association of Middle East Children and Youth Studies Book Award and was short-listed for the Palestine Book Awards. As a resident of the Old City of Jerusalem, Professor Shalhoub-Kevorkian is a prominent local activist. She engages in direct actions and critical dialogue to end the inscription of power over Palestinian children's lives, spaces of death, and women's birthing bodies and lives.

ILAN PAPPÉ: We will discuss aspects of violence experienced by women and children in Palestine, and I know how difficult it is to talk about these issues. Nevertheless, like you, I feel it is crucial not to overlook these aspects of life under occupation and colonization in Palestine.

My first question, therefore, is whether you can tell us about the choices that you made as a scholar, when you decided to look at some of the most brutal, ugliest sides of state brutality and crimes. Not an easy choice for an object of inquiry. Where does it meet your other focus on gender and gender-based violence? Is it your biography from an early part of your life or more recent? Or is it something else altogether?

NADERA SHALHOUB-KEVORKIAN: Let me start by saying that my main concern, as a scholar-activist, was related to how my research disrupts violence, in particular settler-colonial violence, and especially as a feminist researcher. How can I examine, expose, and unpack settler-colonial structures? How can I talk about the systems that are predicated on recurring patterns of domination and violence that invade and destroy bodies, communities, land, and psychic knowledges of otherized groups, whether Black, Brown, Indigenous, or Palestinian? My theorization and research methodologies are born from the bodies and flesh, the wounding, the relationship and abilities of those living, loving, dying, and being killed by the Israeli system.

To position myself right from the beginning, I'm speaking to you from the Old City of Jerusalem—where daily military occupation, ethnic cleansing, apartheid, dispossession, and kill-ability is confronted with Palestinians' livability, togetherness, joy, love, and growing solidarity here and around the world. I'm speaking to you from inside the Old City of Jerusalem, yet out of place while being *in* our place, in our homeland. We are exilic subjects, exiled at home, and it's almost like a waiting game, with the Zionists waiting for us to die, to leave, to disappear, to evaporate. We are not really out of place, but witnessing the unending refusal of the Palestinians to accept uprooting as the only mode of maintaining the settler state.

My research is a decolonial process that is historically situated but present-focused and futuristic. It's untethered from my being here, living here—from Haifa where I was born to the Old City of Jerusalem. It's witnessing, it's looking at what happened to my people, my places, and the various movements that are changing things. It is based on those who seldom have the right to narrate, when such narrations are anti-oppressive. As in the case of schoolgirls who are speaking against sexual harassment by the Israeli military and the security police, or the voices of birthing mothers resisting demographic dispossession. And the voices of those who build their continuity and power amidst the housing demolitions.

Research and the landscape of knowledges and activism is one of the many interconnected sides of anticoloniality and decoloniality. And decoloniality in my academic production, feminist activism, and writing tries to eliminate the manifestation of settler-colonial violence that persists via the occupation of land, the occupation of mind, the occupation of families, psyche, and even of the senses.

My research is not a reaction to settler colonialism, or an attempt to recover a settler-colonial past. It's an ongoing orientation toward knowing and being, influenced by many amazing critical scholars from the [Global] South, including Edward Said's analysis in "Permission to Narrate," where he taught us that facts do not stand on their own. They require narratives and authorization. Unfortunately, the Palestinian narrative is not authorized, which means that Palestinians are constantly trying to gain the permission to narrate.

So my work is looking at those issues and unpacking violence, while thinking, "How can a 'terrorist,' let alone a woman academic 'terrorist,' narrate academically and convincingly without being authorized?" It's a mode of de-linking from hegemonic coloniality with an attempt to imagine a future—not "another" future. Because what I see here in the space around me is really the life of an orphan. All I see in my place, in my time, in the geography, and in my research is very gloomy.

I study Palestine and the manifestation of the colonial project, with its psychosocial and gendered manifestations. My writing and activism emphasize the way in which settler-colonial violence, theft, securitized surveillance, and military occupation of land and life results in ontological and epistemic violence. It results in psychological harm, and here I refer to the amazing work of comrades in South Africa. In my work as a sociolegal scholar and mental health criminologist, I learned that by legitimizing borders and boundaries of disciplines, I risk continuing that colonial violence, knowledge, and being. Colonialism, as Fanon taught us all, is about division of the world into compartments without borders patrolled and policed by structural violence. Decolonial research requires digging deep into the white-stream academic institutions as hubs of epistemic violence and centers for knowledge production. And instead centering the perspective of women, of men, of children, of community—centering the voices of the living and the dead.

ILAN PAPPÉ: Let's unpack some of what you are disrupting in your work. As you said, one of the important things is gendered violence and violence against women in the Israeli policy. I think we were all made aware of it, even in a nonscholarly way, in the wake of the Israeli assassination of the Al Jazeera journalist Shireen Abu Akleh.

Your work details how women in Palestine suffer from more than one source of violence. We will talk about at least of two of them: Israeli oppression and Palestinian patriarchy, and the connection between them. Let us focus first on the impact of Israeli policy. Is there a particular Israeli violence directed against the women, which is different from or similar to other targeted groups? How common is this violence in what you call "conflict zones"?

My feeling is that somehow Israel created the impression that gender-based violence is not a feature of violence that is relevant to the Zionist movement or the Jewish state, either in the past or in the present. How true is this self-image that quite a lot of people in the world accept?

NADERA SHALHOUB-KEVORKIAN: It's worth emphasizing that feminist scholarship on Palestine has often traced different effects of colonial power, especially its invasion of the intimate, its silencing, its disciplining, and its surveillance of the colonized. To me, Shireen Abu Akleh's assassination is state criminality. Most studies on gender-based violence do not look at state crime or state criminality and its gender. State settler-colonial violence, her assassination and Israel's lies around it—the violence of the state that followed—is all about necropolitical violence that usually those in power do not talk about.

I just completed a special volume titled *The Cunning of Gender Violence: Geopolitics and Feminism* with my dear friends Professor Lila Abu-Lughod from Columbia University and Professor Rema Hammami from Birzeit. In the book we explore the dynamic political and institutional circuits that GBVAW (Gender-Based Violence and Violence against Women) inhabits, the way it traverses, consolidates, and animates. My contribution to the volume exposes the way that gendered violence is central to state-making and sustaining state power. Other studies, for example Nadje Al-Ali in Iraq, describe how gender is used by states and who also claim to "save" women. Lila Abu-Lughod writes about whether Muslim women "need saving" in her work, and Rema Hammami discusses how humanitarian intervention dramatizes violence against women to invade the state and to invade the otherized, as they are used by the state.

My argument is that state violence can even work through humanitarian registers of saving, of sympathy. Addressing this apparatus of GBV (Gender-Based Violence) and violence against women from *a state crime perspective* allows me to detect the ways in which state violence works through gender. And it allows feminists to engage with the violence of state institutions and the law, to draw from Indigenous conceptualizations of justice, to examine everyday life and politics, and to go beyond the state and its local and global capitalist economy. When we explain the cunning of gender violence, we say that it can be integral to the working of state power, whether wielded in its biopolitical governance—such as Israel's demographic, citizenship, and family reunification laws—or subtending authoritarian or necropolitical projects of exclusion, expulsion, and slow deportation.

In the case of Shireen Abu Akleh, the violent event began when an Israeli sniper fired directly at her in Jenin Camp. But later that day, her family gathered in Jerusalem, here in Beit Hanina. They were terrified by the news, but the Israeli military and the Israeli police entered their home, not to give respect to the deceased but to dictate the funeral procession. The Israeli police threatened Shireen's family with severe consequences if a Palestinian flag were to appear. And Shireen's family members were sitting in shock. The next day at the doors of the French Hospital in Jerusalem, Palestinians gathered from different places, from the Naqab, Nazareth, al-Lydd—and the same happened.

So Shireen's body and the body of Fatima Hajiji, who came from Tulkarm to Jerusalem and was shot and killed in Bab al-Amoud [Damascus Gate], are used and abused as *women's* bodies. And they become a tool of oppression and serve the settler-colonial project, in which the Zionist power is sustained through pain, through dispossession, through the flesh. Israel's necropolitics and the state's ability to wield biopower in the subjugation of death over human bodies and populations for the purpose of preserving state sovereignty and its authority is fascinating. And it was clearly apparent in Shireen Abu Akleh's case.

I recall walking around the Old City so many times that day, as if telling the streets not to worry, that I'm there. I kept seeing students and people gathering by the Melkite Catholic cemetery and church—a church that I was married in. It was hard to see her body being brought to a church where I left as a bride, and then she left as a dead body. It was really a painful scene. The fact that Israel did not honor dead bodies was so clear that a psychic and collective process of uplifting happened among us, creating songs and chanting. One of the very important ones was "Raise your voice. Raise your voice. It's better to die than to be undignified and stepped on."[1]

But in that moment of devastation, in that moment where Palestinians tried psychologically to expand the home space and mourn Shireen Abu Akleh, in that space of heartbreak, of rage, of shock, of grief, Palestinian dead bodies were not regarded as human. And this is where you see that the gendered aspect is so immersed and interlocked in different aspects of settler-colonial violence. But again, at the same time, Palestinians refused to become exilic subjects at home. They insisted on engaging in practices to repair and to mourn her—despite the Zionist threat, despite the actual harm, despite the million checkpoints. So from one side you have Palestinians chanting "Raise your hand, raise your voice. If you don't chant, you will end up dying,"[2] which is again speaking to necropolitics and the economy of life and death among Palestinians. You see the system trying to asphyxiate and silence us.

This is the gendered nature of settler colonialism and its racialized regime, which I understand as a product of the politico-social and psycho-economic system—when policing, governance, and tear gas are pouring into our homes, our offices, our schools. This is what I study. I study and live in a settler reality, so my studies *name* the settler-colonial reality and its gendered effects. And I have really learned from many feminists around the world. Although I look at Palestine, you see this violence against women in different conflict zones—sometimes counted, sometimes documented, but sometimes totally invisible. So I have learned from different legal scholars like Ratna Kapur, Leti Volpp, Patricia Williams, and Sherene Razack. Also Françoise Vergès, mental health workers like my colleague Stephanie Wahab, or philosophers such as Achille Mbembe, Ann Laura Stoler, and Judith Butler. My work tries to engage with scholars from the South and the North, but at the same time it is situated—and my first teachers are my people here in Palestine.

ILAN PAPPÉ: An additional mental dimension of the Israeli settler-colonial project is surveillance, which you see daily in Jerusalem and through your research. Some of your major works focus on this issue, which aligns with what you were just saying about a comprehensive Israeli wish to control not only the living but also the dead, and not just the bodies but also psyches.

Those of us who visit Jerusalem are aware of the CCTV control of every corner in the Old City. But it seems that in your research, you see this technology as a small part of a wider phenomenon [of policing] and settler-colonial violence—Jewish marches, graffiti, and festivals are no less important in imposing what you call the "occupation of the senses" on local Palestinians. It becomes an attempt by the colonizer to police every aspect of human action and feelings. And I feel that people abroad are not always aware of how systematic this occupation or colonization of the senses by Israel is. You can see it in the compact reality and environment of the Old City in Jerusalem. Can you expand about this "occupation of the senses" as a field of inquiry in your work? Can you tell us about its manifestation in Jerusalem?

NADERA SHALHOUB-KEVORKIAN: It was a major struggle to write this article, because even scholars who are close to me challenged the concept of "the occupation of the senses" and "aesthetic violence." No one understood that every time I saw the Flag Parade, the music festival, or the Light Festival, it was so heavy on my heart. And every time I tried to explain that these events are about deleting, erasing the Palestinians and rewriting history—the history is only of one people. I felt that the politics of *viscerality* played a major role in my work on the occupation of the senses.

By occupation of the senses, I refer to the technologies that are managing the language, the sight, the sound, the time, the light. Come here and listen to the darkness, look at the light and the space in the colony! It is the administration of who acts, who speaks, who gives birth and how. Who walks, who moves, who drives where and how. What kind of language, music, smells, marches, colors, cultures, and scenes are promoted or inscribed over spaces. It goes back to the analysis of settler colonialism. Settler colonialism is a structure not an event, as Patrick Wolfe told me. It is built on the logic of elimination, and it is about the eviction of the native and the indigenization of the settler.

My inquiry is concerned with the ways in which the settler colony uses sensory stimuli in a confrontational manner with the aim of invading the experience of the colonized, producing exclusivity and hegemony on the basis of one culture, one religion, one national and security claim. When analyzing the occupation of the senses, I consider aesthetics and symbolic violence against the Palestinians in occupied East Jerusalem with the focus on visual displays of power, such as the state-sponsored Jerusalem Light Festival or the "price tag" where they spray slogans on walls. I discuss the marches and the parades, and I look at the way that visuals intersect with other stimuli—what we smell is skunk water and what we see is Jewish history, Jewish parades, the Israeli flag, and the Star of David on settler houses in Silwan. The occupation of the senses produces a more complete regime of colonial control over Palestinian sensory experience and over Jews who are visiting.

I deal with the biopolitical and necropolitical manifestations. I discuss demographics and birth in the colonial context, and I argue that the dynamic of occupation extends to the experiences of pregnant and birthing mothers, penetrating their senses but also their wombs. And I conduct fieldwork with children who have been shot in the eyes, or blinded by live fire—I consider the maiming of children's sight by Israeli soldiers as contributing to the occupation of the senses.

At my dentist in Isawiya, I met a five-year-old boy who was shot in the eye. He was telling me about the pain, that he left the bus and was running because he was very hungry. He was running to his mother because he thought that she had prepared food, but suddenly he was shot in the eye. For an hour he described how his eye still hurts him. They operated under his cheek and now he suffers from severe headaches, wears eyeglasses, and so on. By the end of listening to him for one hour I said, "So, what should we do now?" He looked at me and said, "I won't get hungry anymore."[3]

When you listen to a child who was shot in the eye and he thought that maybe it happened because he was very hungry and rushed to his house, it makes you think about the occupation of the senses. In my writing, I also look at dead bodies—Israel's withholding of Palestinian dead bodies and the way it is a necro-penological element. Again, you need to remember that I'm a criminologist. I look at penal law and withholding dead bodies such as that of Hassan Manasra. Hassan Manasra was fifteen years old, and I recall the discussions in his house for seven months, trying to free his dead body from an Israeli refrigerator. His mother kept telling me that she feels him, that her hands are frozen because he is frozen. She hears him calling to her all night long, "Please release me from this freezer." Or the case of Mohammed Abu Khdeir. When I look at the necro-penology, the biopolitics, and the occupation of the senses that invade the visceral, I conclude by proposing that criminologists and criminological approaches should take sensory violence into consideration. If I would call for an abolition, I would call for the abolition of violence against the senses here.

ILAN PAPPÉ: And you actually go beyond that. In a recent edited book titled *When Politics Are Sacralized*, you describe these surveillance policies and this comprehensive control of Palestinian life and dead bodies as part of the settlers' "security theology." A theology that has strong racist and misogynist undertones, as you explored in your 2015 book *Security Theology, Surveillance and the Politics of Fear*. Why did you use the term "theology" to name these policies of security, surveillance, and fear? Can you say more about the gendered aspects of both the motivation and the impacts of the security theology?

NADERA SHALHOUB-KEVORKIAN: In my book in 2015, I looked at security as a theology, where the theology also refers to the Biblical theology. Because when you talk to people in Hebron or in Jerusalem, their reaction was, "Well, God gave us the land." That is the theology from one side, and you also have the security that is religiously framed in Israel. In the book I drew from everyday aspects of Palestinian victimization, survival, life, and death. And I move from the local to the global because the book talks about the political economy of fear. I introduce and analyze the politics of fear and the security theology within the Israeli settler-colonial logic of elimination. And I examine violent acts committed against Palestinians in the name of "security necessities," considering how such "necessities" demand surveillance. The cameras, the control, the police, the military, the surveillance that we see and the surveillance that we don't see.

The surveillance of certain racialized bodies maintains and reproduces the Israeli political economy of fear, which is built on the fear of losing their right—because "God gave them the land." By opening the analytical horizon to the voices of those who keep existing, I explore how Israeli theologies and ideologies of fear, of security, and Biblical claims can obscure violence and power dynamics while perpetuating existing power structures that aim at the liquidation of all truths. This is what I see if I use Fanon's work, which is embedded in colonized people's existence under a specific structure of oppression—here namely Israeli settler colonialism.

In order to read and understand such untruths as well as daily efforts to liquidate them, I rely on feminist analysis that invokes the intimate politics of everydayness and remains connected to political constraints. The politics of everydayness enables a feminist reading of the settler-colonial regime—its sovereignty and its mode of working. And it directs our awareness to the mundane, routine, intimate, private sites where power is both reproduced and contested. Think about a sniper's rifle. In my book I have a chapter called "Israel in My Bedroom," where I highlight the case of a woman in Sheikh Jarrah who says that the sniper "keeps on trying with his dot"—the red dot from his sniper's rifle continually invades her bedroom.

This attention to the mundane, to routine activities, reiterates the feminist notion that the personal is political. And it alludes to the way in which the everyday is a space for oppression and domination, but also for subversion and creativity. I see this clearly in Palestine. The branding as "security risk" justifies numerous interventions into the most intimate rhythm of the everyday—to delay or deny passage to pregnant women in labor at checkpoints, to deny medical assistance, to hinder family reunification, to demolish homes, to deny dead bodies the right to a dignified burial. It invades every single aspect.

The book really argues that in order to maintain a productive global and local industry and political economy that produces and reproduces fear, Israel's security was transformed into a religion. Into a theology. This theology has been combined with the Zionist Biblical claim of Jewish birth right and "the promised land" to create a new settler-colonial theology in Israel. The Biblical claims of Jews' chosen-ness and return serves Israel's narrative as a legitimate and sovereign state. They also work to cast Israeli violence against Palestinians as a security necessity. So the discursive collapse of Biblical and security claims work to exonerate racist structures, to mask state violence through the Biblical security prism and naturalize the dispossession of Palestinians.

To develop this analysis further, I worked on a major project with my colleague Nadim Rouhana and we published a book titled *When Politics Are Sacralized.* In the book we draw comparisons, for example, with India, Sri Lanka, and Northern Ireland. You can see sacralized politics being used in different ways. Through case studies, including Zionism, we could talk about the effect of this theology. Think about one person who needs to first face security and then the claim that "well, it's God." How can this be challenged? You see the power of Palestinians in refusing, refuting, and defying.

Another example is the watch towers, like those in Bab al-Amoud. Israel was bragging, "Here we have the watch towers, the cameras. We check. We can hear. Even if fifty people speak together, we can divide the voices and hear exactly what they said." I sit on the stairs of Bab al-Amoud to watch kids walking to school and when I ask them about the towers they call them "the killing boxes." This is resistance, just naming those so-called watch towers as killing boxes. Those are boxes where soldiers sit with their rifles and the aim is to kill and not to protect, not to secure, not even to listen to what God has told them.

ILAN PAPPÉ: Moving away from the diagnosis to the prognosis, let's talk about agency. You are a local activist—there is no rest for such activism if the habitat you live in is your space of activism, when daily, if not hourly, things happen that demand your attention as an activist. I have two related questions in this respect.

First, would you mind sharing with us your own experience of living in the Old City? When we last met, you were kind enough to share with me the walk you take from the Jaffa Gate to your home— not an ordinary journey by any means, although it is less than a mile long. Each walk, which is a mundane action, is probably also a walk of activism, defiance, and agency. Many of our students and the people with us tonight are interested in how to fuse activism with scholarship—your activism and inquiry are corresponding. Do you worry about accusations that your work lacks scholarly "objectivity" or professionalism? Or do you see such a fusion as an asset and part of the struggle for decolonization in Palestine?

Second, we would like you to say more about how you view the present modes of resistance against all these aspects that are hidden or less hidden, but are comprehensive and brutal. How do you see this mode of resistance, in Palestine in general and more specifically in Jerusalem? What are its prospects in the future? From what you tell us, this sounds like an unbearable existence—and surely there is a limit to how much people are willing to tolerate. Yet this has been happening for quite a while.

I am interested in agency here—your own and your observations of resistance.

NADERA SHALHOUB-KEVORKIAN: Let me start with my walk in the Old City. I live here, I shop here, my kids went to school here. And what I see is so much power. So much power. I see it in produce sellers, I see it in children, I see it in their acts. My activism is inseparable from my academic work and my observations. Let me give you an example, because we mentioned Shireen Abu Akleh. For a long time, I was looking at settler violence in different places in the Old City. Settler violence is greater in some spaces because they are there with their own security people, including those who are hidden.

I work a lot with Silwan and one thing I notice is children's play—al-ghumayda or "hide-and-seek." Playing hide-and-seek says, "This is my place. I know every corner." You don't see Jewish settler kids playing hide-and-seek in the middle of the street in our neighborhood or in Haret al-Sa'diyya, Aqabat el-Battikh, or Silwan. Hide-

and-seek itself gave me so many ideas about what happens between the Zionist game and the refusal and defiance of these children.

Following the assassination of Shireen Abu Akleh, I went to Haret al-Sa'diyya and there was a little girl, seven or eight years old, and a large group of soldiers. The soldiers were talking and suddenly she started calling her friend in a loud voice, "Fattoum! Fattoum! Come play hide-and-seek!" And she looked at the soldiers, telling them in a loud voice, "If you killed Shireen Abu Akleh, do you think I'm not going to play hide-and-seek?" This is what she said. "If you fill the graveyards with our bones, do you think we're not going to play hide-and-seek?" And she kept on calling Fattoum.

Listen, just hearing her voice. This is a voice of clear defiance, of resistance, of refusal of power. I look at those things that maybe many people would pass and wouldn't notice—her voice and her call for Fattoum. But her call for Fattoum! Lara and Stephen Sheehi's book *Psychoanalysis under Occupation: Practicing Resistance in Palestine* takes us beyond what we hear. It takes us to new spaces of analysis. It looks at what goes on in the psyche, in the *nafs*, as they say in their book. My work is a fusion between the analytical and the emotional, for I am concerned with affective dimensions and what happens to kids when they play hide-and-seek—when they're calling Fattoum while saying, "Yes, we know that you kill us, but we will continue playing." I am concerned with the affective states exhibited by racialized subjects and produced through political processes of racialization. I looked at Mohammed Abu Khdeir's burning. I looked at Ahmad Manasra, who was arrested when he was thirteen years old. We started a major campaign for his release, but he is still in solitary confinement. This is a *Zionist* settler-colonial regime. It is similar to what happens in other contexts, but what happens here is beyond imagination.

My work looks at structural racism, the collective witnessing of lynching—of Eyad al-Hallaq, two minutes from my house—slow death, and the killing of children. We are attempting the work of mental health with Palestine-Global Mental Health Network. We are working with Palestine Solidarity Campaign, Cafe Palestine, Black Lives Matter, and Standing Rock. We are working with our comrades in South Africa, trying to understand but also respect children's walk to school, children's language—how they speak *life* when the system speaks death and unchilding. To me, hide-and-seek exposes what the cameras, the arrests, and the tapping does not.

Gayatri Chakravorty Spivak

COLONIALITY, SUBALTERNITY, AND REVOLUTION IN OUR TIME

May 26, 2022

Gayatri Chakravorty Spivak is University Professor in the Humanities at Columbia University. Her books are *Myself Must I Remake* (1974), *Of Grammatology* (1976; translation of Derrida's *De la grammatologie*, with critical introduction), *In Other Worlds* (1987), *Outside in the Teaching Machine* (1993), *A Critique of Postcolonial Reason* (1999), *Other Asias* (2003), *An Aesthetic Education in the Era of Globalization* (2013), and *Readings* (2014). She has won the Kyoto Prize (2012) and the Padma Bhushan (2013). She holds fifteen honorary doctorates. "Can the Subaltern Speak?" has become a worldwide classic. She is finishing a book on W. E. B. Du Bois and editing a hitherto untranslated exchange between Giulia and Tatiana Schucht and the incarcerated Antonio Gramsci. She is active in rural education, ecological agriculture, the role of subaltern languages in the field of development, and the fate of future generations.

ILAN PAPPÉ: Thank you for your time in the midst of a very hectic schedule, Gayatri. We began talking about this conversation when you were in rural India, and now you are on the brink of beginning a tour of lectures and meetings that will take you to the Gulf, Africa, and beyond. My first question is whether you can tell us a bit of what you have been engaged with in India during these past few months?

GAYATRI CHAKRAVORTY SPIVAK: I do not have much "all-India" involvement beyond signing petitions, showing solidarity, and movement connections. My work is teaching and training for the development of a pedagogy that will develop the intuitions of democracy in the children of the largest sector of the electorate: the outcasts and tribals. They don't call themselves "Dalits" now, that's more in southern India, but the name is being picked up because politicians are using them. I have four elementary schools for the last thirty-six years and I also work on the development of ecological agriculture. I work with girls and boys, women and men, from a gender-sensitive practice. I've also recently been asked to work with the ministry of education in West Bengal, which is my home state. But there I'm feeling my ropes because I'm a Rosa Luxemburg–style social democrat: if the state calls me, I will go. It's both medicine and poisonous. I've been involved on lower levels with the state for a very long time, but now this is the ministry. There I'm really learning how I can work with a state like West Bengal.

ILAN PAPPÉ: There is your theoretical writing about education, and also you have this very practical experience in educating. I wonder whether the things you are doing in the schools are associated with what you refer to as "holistic education"—Marx's idea of educating for citizenship.

Can you elaborate on this and how it might differ from concepts such as "unlearning"? Where do we carry out this kind of education? You mentioned that part of what you do is work within the national educational system, which is a model you can follow in many other countries. But not in authoritarian regimes or in settler colonial regimes like Israel, where probably we need to seek parallel, alternative, and maybe even clandestine ways of educating the educators. Whichever way we choose, it seems you are charting for us an activist path that might help us to go beyond academic conversations on inhumanities in our ivory tower. Am I reading too much into the concept of holistic education and how global or local your experience can be?

GAYATRI CHAKRAVORTY SPIVAK: When I was using the word "holistic," what I actually meant was no class apartheid in education, so that it goes from subaltern to elite in a certain way so that people really don't know anything about the bottom layer.

But I do not work within the national education system. I teach the national curriculum so that my students can enter the mainstream, if necessary. But the situation of the subaltern, groups on the fringes of history, is not generalizable. Every subaltern situation calls for its own tactic, strategy, policy, et cetera.

As for "unlearning," it is the privileged unlearning their privilege. I think that is very narcissistic. It is better to use the privilege for subalternist intervention, although not as a sustained top-down policy. But unlearning false information in textbooks is absolutely essential. One must see what form the unlearning takes, how it appears. If we are just focused on unlearning our own privilege, first of all, it never happens. And second of all, it's that kind of narcissistic self-involvement that you see in how bourgeois ideologues talk about themselves, as if they're the example of the most radical stuff, and how they ask questions. I find that "unlearning of my privilege" boring and I think privilege should be used, although not in a sustained way. But unlearning false information in textbooks? Absolutely essential. We do it all the time.

ILAN PAPPÉ: As you observed, "the subaltern" is a term that is at the times misused, sometimes even abused. In particular, there seems to be a tendency to ignore the underpinning Marxist analysis in your work on the topic. To a certain extent, we probably exhausted the discussion about the validity and usefulness of the term, had it not been for the tragic fact that this century introduced us to many more and new subalterns.

My first question in this regard: Is the definition dynamic enough to include not only the obvious new subalterns, namely the life-seekers and refugees of this century, but also those who are the citizens of settler-colonial countries, such as the Palestinian minority in Israel whose citizenry does not immunize them from subalternity? And a second interconnected question: In your mind, is subalternity still a phenomenological term—unlike class or gender—that enables us to analyze inhumanity but not represent its victims or engage with their predicaments? Is this a fair approach to the concept, after so many years?

GAYATRI CHAKRAVORTY SPIVAK: Well, I do think that "Can the Subaltern Speak?" was a beginning. I was having a certain kind of very metropolitan crisis about being taken to be an expert on French deconstruction. It was really a bit bogus because one is so de-skilled and one is always obliged to speak about the place of origin, et cetera, that at that point I should have realized it was good fortune to be taken as an expert on deconstruction! But that was when I wrote two pieces, "Three Women's Texts and a Critique of Imperialism" and "Can the Subaltern Speak?" But "Can the Subaltern Speak?" was really a beginning, and then things changed.

When the rights of citizenship cannot be accessed, as in the case of Palestine, that is certainly subalternity. We are doing it at home and we are doing it in India: taking away citizenship through various modes from Muslims who have lived there forever but do not have the papers. How would they prove it? That is subalternization, taking away rights of citizenship. And when our Palestinian colleagues suffer absolute discrimination in international professional travel, that is subalternization. Subalternity and subalternization are two different things, again asking for different kinds of strategies. The subaltern is certainly also racialized and gendered. We certainly need to engage with them—not just to learn from them how to teach, but also to consolidate infrastructure so that someday they can be heard.

If you just keep it as an idea, or especially if people come forward and say, "I'm a subaltern, I can speak. Hey, listen!" they haven't understood that it's not about self-promotion. Not every kind of suffering or location is subalternity as one can use it—because these are people now who vote! This is why I talked about intuitions of democracy, et cetera. Someone asked me, "How can you do it?" I can't tell you. I'm just failing. I've learned from my mistakes for thirty-six years. Because you don't undo the denial of intellectual labor—which is another condition of subalternity—by just being nice. I'm learning how to learn from failures and not think of them as failures.

It's possible to fail in a certain way with the subaltern in a common enterprise, but intellectual labor cannot be taught. So "how?" is really one of those impatient elite questions. You would not ask me to teach you how to sing in just one session, would you? And it's certainly more complicated, more difficult than playing the piano or singing revolution. Therefore, I would say that, yes, we need to engage it, but engaging with subalternity is not so easy. And anytime we want to represent ourselves as subalterns, we should stop immediately. Frederick Douglass did not represent himself as a subaltern. Remember him.

ILAN PAPPÉ: Let's move to your engagement with history in the widest possible sense of the term. You help professional historians, like myself, to see the importance of theory when writing our historical work. And you use history to clarify a moral, philosophical position.

You are meticulous in your historical research, and my impression is that any point you want to emphasize comes with a historical example—culminating in your upcoming work on W. E. B. Du Bois. Du Bois allows us to build a new genealogy of racism, including what you called in your book *An Aesthetic Education in the Era of Globalization* "low-grade racism." Why do you attach so much importance to concretizing your theoretical arguments with historical examples? Is it a method of widening your readership? Is it a way of maintaining relevance to reality beyond discussive realities? Or is it something different altogether?

GAYATRI CHAKRAVORTY SPIVAK: I have never asked myself, "Why do I always concretize the theoretical?" I'm glad you pointed it out. And, yes, I do! I've never thought to justify this. Maybe it's the literary impulse to turn thinking into learning. I wish I had a couple of hours to talk about this incredibly hard thing—the imaginative activism of entering another space, effacing oneself as far as possible. For example, the last few days in Dakar and before that at the new Mohammed VI Polytechnic University. Having soldiered all my life, I have a strong self-concept, so that begins to interfere! It's a resistance. But the imaginative activism of entering another space, effacing oneself as far as possible, comes out in interaction with historian friends.

I've never thought of the precolonial as a comfort zone, but that's because I come from this caste, Hindu background. "Can the Subaltern Speak?" is not postcolonial—it's a very strong critique of the precolonial. I've taught myself to look for the *universalizable* there, in the precolonial, without universalizing. And to think secularism outside of the colonial story, which I am still trying to do.

I will think about this involvement with history, because it seems to me that history—its truth claims and verifiability—must go hand in hand with the fact that, in the literary, we learn to learn from the unverifiable. In a very difficult way. And the unverifiable is something that helps in the subaltern work because Gramsci's main point is that they do not have access to historiography, which is the difference from the South Asian subaltern studies group.

ILAN PAPPÉ: A different aspect of the way you use history is to my mind more ambivalent, as probably it should be. History is also a reservoir of structures that can reemerge or be called upon by contemporary societies. When you were engaged in Radiating Globality,[1] you and your colleagues noticed the resurgence of precolonial structures you refer to as "the negative outcome of the failure of liberation." But when you discuss secularism and gender in traditional—for absence of a better term—societies while berating what you called "ready-fix feminism," or when you mention the Ottoman Empire, which you beautifully described as "the carrier of an attitude of conflictual co-existence toward religious difference," you seem to have much more respect for precolonial realities and even attitudes.

This is a more ambivalent relationship to precolonial structures. In this respect, I find you are very much attuned to the fascinating contemporary work done by Arab and North African thinkers who conjure the past as an inspiration for alternative models of liberation that will take them out of what they call "the long winter of Arab postcoloniality." They dig into the past, also, to liberate themselves from equating universalism with Westernism, or Eurocentrism, in a search so poetically enunciated by the Tunisian poet Amina Said when she writes, "I issue from my childhood and thus from nowhere else." Is it possible that part of decolonization is also demodernization, if modernization equates across Westernization? Or is it at least a cautious demodernization?

GAYATRI CHAKRAVORTY SPIVAK: If we sat down together, as happened yesterday when I gave the inaugural talk for the Dakar Biennale, we begin to see how much we did agree. Maybe if we sat down together, the agreements would emerge. I was talking to them about why this kind of gesture is potentially a gesture that denies complicity, being folded together. In my work, I began to realize that the left and the right were completely allied—and you cannot do anything without noticing this. I was saying yesterday that there is no nationalist shame in acknowledging collaboration with certain areas of colonialism—very class-fixed, gender-focused. This is a complicated situation. I asked them to look at Flora Shaw's book, *A Tropical Dependency: An Outline of the Ancient History of the Western Sudan with an Account of the Modern Settlement of Northern Nigeria*. This book was written by Flora Shaw—who later married Lugard, the head of Nigeria—and published in 1905. W. E. B. Du Bois's personal copy is broken into nothingness.

When I asked yesterday, most people didn't know the name of this book, which is about the fantastic Ifriqiya Islamic Empire in this area. Shaw was very much *for* this and *against* the Europeans, but she had a kind of racism against the Bantu that generally is still implicit in the Ifriqiya studies—that, for her, the Bantu lived in swamps and were cannibals. And I said to them, "Take a look—this is Du Bois's copy. He certainly knew this book very, very well. And ask yourselves in what way these kinds of implicit attitudes are still ours." As I say, the book came out in 1905.

So I'm not completely comfortable with creating alternative histories. I even said, "Why is that necessary? That's a European

fantasy." Europe is also part of our heritage, but a Europe transformed by us. *This* is what we should investigate—that Europe was
not "standing there by itself," although it was trying to. The person
who spoke after me at the Biennale, Ibrahima Wane, was fantastic on this. He gave *such* concrete examples of the transformation
of Europe through the past centuries. It was Skip's idea—Henry
Louis Gates Jr.—that we should think about. The idea of "signify-
ing": how we are folded together, how we are part of what we critique. And that gives us a much stronger position than the creation
of this binary opposition.

It can be a comfort zone. But that comfort is not the same as
being global together. It's theocracy in India, it's the Silk Road in
China, and it's Europe being interpellated once again as the source
of democratic behavior, when we look at Ukraine.

So it seems to me that we would really need to sit down together
and ask ourselves, "Is this, indeed, what we want, too?" And that
may be because of my historical position. I come from one of the
worst traditions in the world, Aryanism, so therefore perhaps it's
hard for me to step out of it.

ILAN PAPPÉ: As I promised, the last part of our conversation will
focus on Palestine. We will begin with Islamophobia. When the ethnic cleansing of the Rohingya began, as someone who wrote about
the ethnic cleansing of Palestine I was horrified by the similarities
between the two cases in terms of planning, execution, the making of the refugee—and the international silence, which continues
until today. In many ways it is a repeat of the years 1948 to 1950
in Palestine. Is there at the heart of the denial of the Palestinian
ethnic cleansing and refugee problem, and the ethnic cleansing or
genocide of the Rohingya, a strong element of Islamophobia? Particularly when compared with the compassion shown by the West

to so-called white refugees from Ukraine, and notwithstanding the obviously different historical circumstances. Is this something that we need to face and calculate when other people are not raising their voices?

GAYATRI CHAKRAVORTY SPIVAK: I want to share with the audience what I shared with you. I'm like a schoolchild—I write down exam questions. So at three in the morning, I was writing all these answers. And do you know what answer I wrote to this question? "Yes, Islamophobia." All the other answers were long, but I don't think this one requires a long answer. Of course, Islamophobia. And as part of a genocidal 86 percent majority in my country, I have to speak about Islamophobia in a way that carries shame. When the Babri Masjid was destroyed, my mother called me and wept on the phone, saying, "I'm ashamed to be a Hindu." It's the position that one occupies. That's why I say to my students in the villages, "I'm your enemy. I'm good, but you must do without me. My parents were good, but thousands of years of destruction are not undone by two generations. You must do without me."

With the Rohingya situation, this idea of homelessness and statelessness is deeply connected with Islamophobia. This is what is terrifying. Islamophobia gives a certain kind of "-ization" because there's alternative internationality. It goes back to the suppression of Byzantium—it has a very long history and it gets transformed. When we talk about when the Ottoman began to modernize, there was a genocide. So that conflictual coexistence disappeared, just as the conflictual coexistence in my neighborhood disappeared in murderous violence in 1946, when I was four. So this whole business of conflictual coexistence? We know it and it *can* break down. It can become politicized, because religion is such a dangerous thing. That's my childhood experience, that transformation and the killing—with machetes, not guns. Therefore, I would say yes, Islamophobia. It's not something that we can elaborate on without going into a lot of history.

ILAN PAPPÉ: I'm totally persuaded that part of the treatment— the coverage and the discourse—of the Palestinians in the West, especially in the United Kingdom, is marred by Islamophobia. Let's move to modes of resistance in Palestine. We were all shocked by the Israeli assassination of the Al Jazeera journalist Shireen Abu Akleh, whom some of us knew very well. Reporting on the Israeli crimes is one mode of resistance in Palestine, but there are many others. Let me get us both into trouble and talk about suicide bombers, or any young men and women (sometimes teenagers) in Palestine who use their bodies in the struggle in the most tragic way imaginable.

You wrote, "Suicidal resistance is a message inscribed in the body where no other means will get through. It is both execution and mourning, for both self and other, where you die with me for the same cause, no matter which side you are on."[2] From my experience, this issue is one of the most challenging concerns when publicly defending the Palestinian anticolonialist struggle. I fully understand why the Palestinians are using every means at their disposal to stop the destruction of their homeland and their lives.

Do you still feel that way about this mode of resistance? Because I know that people find it unacceptable when you and I write these kinds of things. How do you feel about this or your engagement with the modes of resistance that cannot all be peaceful against a very violent, intent program of destruction, ethnic cleansing, and, at times, genocide?

GAYATRI CHAKRAVORTY SPIVAK: Of course, it's unacceptable if you are just sitting and being reasonable. We are not talking about reasonableness. We are talking about the limits of reasonableness when there is no response from the other side. When the evaluation of human worth turns, we should see who and what produces this conviction. That's the way the subaltern speaks. That's why Mohamed Bouazizi burnt himself in Tunis—there was something that could happen, there *was* a response. He did speak, didn't he? I certainly still think that this is a response in extremis, when no response has been forthcoming, forever. What produces this change, which is completely against reason?

When saying it's "unreasonable," you need to ask, *who* is judging? Anyone like me, who gets such a response where people have read my work, who am I to say it's unreasonable? Of course, from my little corner, it is unreasonable. But I must try to efface myself and go to that place—that's the literary. When I wrote that piece, I won a prize given by George Bush for the most absurd academic piece and I wear it like a crown. It wasn't Noam Chomsky, it wasn't Edward Said, it was me, Gayatri Spivak, because I had tried to understand suicide bombing rather than just dismiss it as unreasonable. So that's what I would say, when no response has been forthcoming. I'm still there.

ILAN PAPPÉ: My final question is about an issue that I know bothers our community of activists and scholars who deal with Palestine in the university. Many of us support the Boycott, Divestment, Sanctions (BDS) movement, and we include the idea of an academic boycott. The counterargument, used even by my good friend Noam Chomsky, is that including a boycott of academic institutions as part of our wish to show solidarity with the Palestinian struggle is a violation of academic freedom. How do you feel about this idea of an attempt by academics who cannot join a liberation army, but feel they are sending a tough message to Israeli academia? It's a dialogue saying, "No, we are not going to have a normal conversation because you are complicit in what's happening in your name, or sometimes collaborating directly with the oppression of the Palestinians."

GAYATRI CHAKRAVORTY SPIVAK: I would say, you cannot buy freedom at any price. And I would also say that when you begin the history of academic freedom with Kant, then you are making a mistake. Look at the academic freedom of the Brahmins. Look at the academic freedom of the Imperial Civil Service in China. Look at a much broader example of *how* academic freedom is bought, how the academy is put in its place where freedom can be bought at any price. I'm with you there. Develop some rage and undo the academy.

In 1899, when Du Bois saw that Sam Hose's knuckles were going to be sold, he stopped and said, "I cannot teach the way I've been teaching. My teaching is now going to be called propaganda." He said this, and then Gramsci says, "The new intellectual must be a *permanent* persuader." They are already saying, "Forget academic freedom." And yours is a position against the state of Israel, its policies and practices. It is not against a religion or race. If you're talking about reasonableness, be reasonable. It's against the policy of a state. I'll be damned if I'm called an antisemite! It's absolutely incorrect to call it antisemitic—it's against a state. These are obvious answers that you would also give.

ILAN PAPPÉ: Yes, but we need to hear it.

GAYATRI CHAKRAVORTY SPIVAK: We need to *say* it. And we need to make it heard.

Yanis Varoufakis

ON CRISIS AND DISOBEDIENCE

May 12, 2021[1]

Yanis Varoufakis is the leader of MeRA25, the political party belonging to DiEM25—Europe's first transnational Pan-European movement. Previously, he served as finance minister of Greece during the first six months of 2015 and, twice, as a member of Greece's parliament. Varoufakis taught economics at the universities of East Anglia, Cambridge, Sydney, Glasgow, Texas, and Athens, where he holds a chair in Political Economy and Economic Theory. He is also honorary professor of Political Economy at the University of Sydney; honoris causa professor of Law, Economics, and Finance at the University College of Turin; visiting professor of Political Economy at King's College, London; and doctor of the University Honoris Causa at University of Sussex. He is the author of a number of best-selling books, including: *Another Now: Dispatches from an Alternative Present* (2020); *Adults in the Room: My Struggle against Europe's Deep Establishment* (2017); *Talking to My Daughter about the Economy: A Brief History of Capitalism* (2017); *And the Weak Suffer What They Must?*

Europe, Austerity and the Threat to Global Stability (2016); and *The Global Minotaur: America, Europe and the Future of the Global Economy* (2015, 2011). His most recent book, *Technofeudalism: What Killed Capitalism*, was published in 2023.

ILAN PAPPÉ: Given the wide scope of your writing and activity, we will be able only to scratch the surface—but we will do our best to cover as much as we can for our community that cares about Palestine, Black history, gender rights, workers' rights, ecology, and decolonization, among many other issues.

While I wanted to have a structured discussion with you, beginning with academia and moving to politics, we cannot ignore what is happening in Palestine right now. To avoid jail, a criminal Israeli prime minister pursues a provocative action against the holiest place for Islam in Palestine and the third-holiest place for Muslims all over the world—trying to ignite a conflict that will allow him to retain power.[2] To do so, he has aligned himself with the right wing in Israel, which dominates Israeli politics today and whose agenda is to fully Judaize Jerusalem and the West Bank through means of another catastrophe, or Nakba.

Brave Palestinian youth were able to thwart some of this plan, defending the homes of the people of Sheikh Jarrah and the sacred Al-Aqsa Mosque. It was clear to everyone that Hamas in Gaza would not remain idle against such a provocation and aggression, nor would large segments of the Palestinian people, who for decades have been living under harsh colonization, brutal occupation, and subject to incremental ethnic cleansing.

We might be in the throes of a third uprising—a third intifada— which includes large segments of the "forgotten Palestinians." These are Palestinians who live inside Israel in unrecognized villages, which are refused basic infrastructure from the state. Or in overcrowded towns prohibited to expand under the apartheid laws of the Israeli regime—a system that causes high levels of unemployment through its policies of segregation. The Palestinian Authority is helpless, the Arab regimes seek normalization rather than commitment, and the West, as always, is silent—and we have not heard much from the Muslim world.

In your opinion, what can we do right now? Should we strengthen our support for the Boycott, Divestment, Sanctions movement? Should we ask for sanctions by governments? What is the next step in our solidarity with the oppressed people of Palestine, given the reality unfolding in the last forty-eight to seventy-two hours?

YANIS VAROUFAKIS: You asked me what we should do, listing a number of things. The answer is: All of the above! We need to engage in the struggle to inform people and call upon governments—even shame them—into taking a position. In the process, we must dissolve the illusion that this is a conflict between two equivalents, which the rest of the world has the right to look upon dispassionately and equidistantly.

I remember something you wrote, maybe twelve years ago, in conjunction with Robert Fisk's prescient comment that unless the Palestinians gain their independence, we will never gain ours. And you wrote, "It seems that even the most horrendous crimes, such as the genocide in Gaza, are treated as disparate events; unconnected to anything that happened in the past, and not associated with any ideology or system."

If you watch the BBC or Sky News today this is how the Palestinian tragedy is presented. There is some factual reporting that so many rockets were fired from Gaza and so many bombs landed in Gaza, and this building was demolished and so many people died. But to quote your poignant words again: "It is as if the whole thing is unconnected to anything that happened in the past and not associated with any system or ideology." This is racism in action. The moment you report on the figures of a one-sided massacre taken out of the context of ongoing and well-planned ethnic cleansing, of pushing a native people off their land, you end up fully complicit in the unspoken genocide. The moment you're allowed to get away without mentioning the underlying white settler project is when you become complicit with the ethnic cleansing being perpetrated.

You can see this most vividly in Germany today, a country populated by people desperately trying to escape a dismal legacy through the tactics of political correctness. Today there is zero information in Germany regarding what's going on in Palestine, how it started, who are doing the killing, or why. Few people know that this latest cycle of violence began when dozens of families were threatened with expulsion from their homes and the destruction of their buildings in East Jerusalem.

Clearly, as you say, we need to do so much on so many fronts. But, for now, let me wear my Greek political hat to convey to you my frustration, even my desperation—indeed, my deep sense of shame and foreboding. You will recall that in 2015 I became a government minister here in Greece—probably the most progressive government in Europe that was the culmination of the massive demonstrations in 2011, the equivalent of Occupy Wall Street in the US or the Indignados in Spain. A broad coalition of progressives gave rise to a movement, which took a small party of the former Eurocommunist left from 4 percent to 40 percent, and thus we stormed the citadels of power. We became the government.

Our manifesto waxed lyrical about our solidarity with the people of Palestine. It targeted racism of every form, including, of course, antisemitism. For six months, we put up a tremendous struggle against the global financial oligarchy. The Greek people rose to the occasion and courageously boosted their support for us from 40 percent to 60 percent. But on the night of July 5th, 2015, when that support manifested itself magnificently in the NO referendum, my then-comrade and prime minister surrendered to the powers-that-be as formally represented by the International Monetary Fund, the European Central Bank, and the European Commission—the infamous Troika.

Now, why am I telling you all this? Because one surrender brings another. The prime minister ostensibly surrendered because he claimed (against my advice and strongly held belief) that we could not successfully resist the financiers' financial demands (i.e., mind-numbing austerity, surrending all remaining public assets to them, abandoning homeowners to the vultures, etc.). Even if one agreed with him that the government had to surrender on the financial front (which, naturally, I did not), the question becomes: But why also surrender on every other front, including the rights of Palestinians? And there's the rub: less than twenty-four hours after my resignation and our government's surrender to the Troika, the Greek foreign minister arrived in . . . Tel Aviv to inaugurate a long, reprehensible love-in between Netanyahu and a Greek "leftist" government that had hitherto pledged solidarity to the Palestinians, as per the sentiments of the vast majority of Greeks.

To my astonishment and horror, my until-a-few-hours-earlier comrades were forging a sordid alliance with Netanyahu's government. Together, they planned to dominate the eastern Mediterranean through a series of aggressive moves, to drill the bottom of the Mediterranean Sea and to construct gas pipelines linking Israel (including Gaza) with Cyprus and Greece—in close association and collaboration with ExxonMobil, the French multinational Total, and, later, Donald Trump's administration.

Speaking personally, the enormous heartache caused by my comrades' abandonment of our people was surpassed only by what

I felt about their cynical and callous abandonment of the Palestinian people, as well as of Israeli progressives languishing under Netanyahu's iron rule. You see, deep down, I wanted to give my comrades the benefit of the doubt, even while disagreeing and falling out with them on financial matters and economic policy. However, the sight of my comrade Alexis Tsipras, the aforementioned prime minister, hobnobbing with Netanyahu, and the manner in which our so-called party of the radical left immediately forgot its solidarity to the Palestinian people, that was the litmus test which my comrades failed, helping me accept that these people were no longer my comrades. They were not just people I disagreed with on matters where rational debate is possible. No, they had mutated into misanthropes.

Four years later, once these former comrades had served the international oligarchy's purpose and had thrown Greece into Israel's geostrategic orbit, they were dispensed with by that same oligarchy. So, in 2019, a rabidly right-wing government (headed by Kyriakos Mitsotakis, who straddles the Trumpist ultraright and the radical center) was elected. During that parliament (2019–2013), the party I helped found in 2018, MeRA25, was represented by nine MPs. One of the first legislative moves I made as parliamentary leader was to table a bill that would have Greece formally recognize the state of Palestine (for symbolic purposes and as a first step toward a UN-led effort to end Israel's apartheid). During that speech, I looked at my former Syriza comrades in the eye and asked: "Will you support this bill recognizing the state of Palestine? If not," I continued, when I noticed they were avoiding eye contact, "how do *you* propose that we restore Greece's support for the Palestinian people?" All I got was a loud silence. And so it was that, in 2023, both Syriza and MeRA25 lost seats in a twin general election that can be described as the left's Waterloo—which makes perfect sense, since our people needed to punish a left that, after having inspired them in 2015, dumped them back into their debtors' prison and, for good measure, abandoned all its principles, as evidenced by the ugly sight of the Tsipras-Netanyahu love-in.

As we know, this kind of silence that I faced that day in Greece's parliament from my former Syriza comrades is the greatest vindication of the crime being perpetrated. It is a guilty silence. That attempt to take an equidistant position is the loudest vote of confidence in Mr. Netanyahu in particular and the Israeli apartheid system in general. Our struggle in Greece today is to reignite the movement against racism, including antisemitism, while at the same time bringing news of the apartheid policies practiced in Israel to the court of public opinion. I am pleased that Human Rights Watch delivered their report on Israel's apartheid. I feel personally indebted to B'Tselem and to other comrades in Israel for raising the question of apartheid. This is what we're trying to do in Germany, with our MERA25 party there, a country where you are almost immediately silenced as an antisemite if you dare challenge the right of Israel to commit any crime against humanity it fancies, if you dare speak out against Israel's apartheid. It is quite preposterous: if you oppose ethnic cleansing, apartheid, mass murder, genocide you are immediately branded an antisemite and a "terrorist enabler." So you are precisely right: we need to fight on many different fronts, at all levels, simultaneously, ceaselessly, night and day.

I'm sorry for taking so long to answer, but this really hurts. Greece used to be quite solidly supportive of, and in solidarity with, the Palestinian people. This is no longer so. We've been defeated by the oligarchy and lured into a false sense of protection from Turkish expansionism by the promise of an invincible (utterly fictional, of course) Greek-Israeli defense pact. As if Israel would lift even a finger to assist Greece if Turkey invaded one of our Aegean islands!

ILAN PAPPÉ: I'm glad you're saying it, because, as you know, if you ask the Israeli foreign minister or foreign ministry diplomats which European countries are the best allies of Israel at this moment, unfortunately Greece would be one of them. But when I come to talk in Athens, I notice that civil society is still very much pro-Palestinian. And in that respect, we still have hope that politics from above in Greece will return to what they used to be. Because Palestinians need every possible ally, in the Mediterranean and in southern Europe—places near to Palestine and the struggle of the Palestinians.

Before deciding to begin tonight with the crisis in Palestine, I actually hoped to start with academia, which is the place many of us come from. I know that at the height of your political career, you would sneak back to academia whenever you could and in many ways examine the relevance of your former home, which was the discipline and department of economics.

It seems that while you were happy to be in a comfort zone, at the same time, revisiting your local sanctuary filled you with frustration. Economics, the discipline, seemed to be decoupled from the economic and political realities of our world. It seems that economic departments in the UK, US, and many other places underrate the importance of the *history* of economics. That they are fascinated with purist models examined in laboratories where space, time, and debt are disturbing variants that would not be considered, in order to preserve the pretended predicative power of economic theory.

The experts teaching economics have dismally failed again and again to provide any valid prediction, mainly by disregarding ethical and ideological considerations that are painted as disruptive to scientific research. This is evident particularly on the eve of spasms in the capitalist system. The way economics is taught and researched still has not changed today. As a historian who is aware that I can easily argue and counterargue with myself using the very same facts—realizing that the different versions, or narratives, would stem primarily from external factors such as my moral positionality—I can fully empathize with the humble recognition that economics, like the discipline of history, is not a science. While both disciplines have crucial elements of empirical study (facts, methods, and models), the end product, be it prediction or historical analysis, is the outcome of "nonscientific" elements as much as it is of the empirical evidence gathered from the laboratory or the archives.

This position is not easy to adopt. It invites politics, ideology, ethics, and morality to enter our world of scholarly work through the front door. It challenges the claim that they are successfully blocked at the gates of the university by academic apparatuses. Such an invitation is still regarded as a heresy in many academic circles, either because people believe it is still possible to be objective, or because such a stance could dry funding for our research—from governments unwilling to support research that contradicts their policies, or corporations reluctant to fund research that undermines their interests.

Am I presenting a position that you identify with? If so, do you see any hope for the discourse of *plurality* rather than the discourse of "proof" as being able to guide future research and teaching in economics? Do you see any change in the way economics is being taught, researched? And what kind of change would you like to see on the part of academia in dealing with economy, political economy, and other issues familiar to you as a politician, a theorist, as an activist?

YANIS VAROUFAKIS: I wholeheartedly endorse your view of economics. And I will take it further. Do I see any prospects of academic economics becoming more relevant, more sophisticated in their approach to capitalism, more cultured, indeed, civilized? No, I don't.

In whichever university I have taught, I have always chosen to teach the first semester of the first year of introductory economics—my attempt to deprogram the students before they proceed to the "harder" stuff. In my classes, I try to teach the parallel evolution of capitalism and of our *ideas about* capitalism—to demonstrate how capitalism and our undersanding (or theory) of capitalism coevolved. Why did Adam Smith write *The Wealth of Nations* in 1776? Why wasn't it written a hundred years earlier? So I focus on the historical necessity of shedding light on events that seemed indecipherable.

Take, for instance, the decoupling of political power from economic power that only occurred as capitalism was rising up. For the first time ever, some people acquired enormous economic power, but they didn't have any political power—the merchants, the first industrialists. Then I move on to explain why economists like David Ricardo suddenly turned against landowners, even though he was one himself! I show why the concept of economic rent had to be invented. Why did Karl Marx become Karl Marx? Why was he writing about the fluctuations of the economic cycle in the first volume of *Capital*? And most importantly, why did economics, from the middle of the nineteenth century, become transformed from a holistic, organic study of the capitalist system to a piecemeal, mathematized, static model resembling primitive classical mechanics? Why was there no room in economics deparments after that transformation for minds like Jeremy Bentham, John Stuart Mill, or Karl Marx—people with a strong ethical compass, approaching the economic system organically, as an evolving entity?

Today's economic textbooks pretend to engage with the large questions: "What is it that gives rise to wealth creation?" "How is income distributed?" "What is the mechanism by which competition leads to innovation, innovation leads to capital accumulation, capital accumulation leads to investment, investment leads to technical progress, technical progress leads to social ruptures, and so on?" Alas, the textbooks from which youngsters learn economics today only pay lip service to these questions. In reality, these big questions have not been tackled in any substantive way since the first classical economists did so—people who did not even call themselves economists. And here is the irony: Once economics became professionalized, and the first chairs in economics were inaugurated after economics' great transformation to a third-rate version of classical mechanics (neoclassical economics, as it is now called), form has replaced substance and the large questions are routinely sidelined. What has taken their place? The answer is a huge amount of intellectual effort to treat capitalism as if it is a phenomenon like the motion of the planets in a Newtonian sense, whereby a system of equations needs to be solved so that you can work out how the whole thing works, operates, functions.

And suddenly this professionalization process created the modern academic economist, embedded in the great universities in Europe. Except that this type spoke a language that Adam Smith, John Stuart Mill, David Ricardo, Karl Marx, and the rest would not recognize. Indeed, they would have no time for it even if they did recognize it. Why did this happen? What's behind this transformation? What sociology of knowledge, of the profession, explains its physics envy?

My answer is that economics, as it evolved over the last one hundred and seventy years, is a most peculiar failure—an inverse Darwinian process. According to Darwin, evolution involves two parallel mechanisms: a process of adaptation that favors the capacity to remain in tune with one's environment and a second process that throws out mutations which test the evolutionary process' stability.

Together, the two mechanisms ensure that the more successful adaptations (and the ones that are not destabilized by random mutations) are the ones that prevail. In economics, the opposite holds: the *less* relevant the model is to really existing capitalism, the greater the academic power it imparts to the economist who comes up with that model. Now how did such an absurd dynamic emerge?

The greatest utility for academic economics comes from appearing to be the queen of the social sciences, with economists luxuriating in the image of the nearest there is to a social physicist. To gain an upper hand vis-à-vis anthropology, sociology, and other disciplines, economists found it remarkably profitable to present themselves as the "scientists of society." To this purpose, they need to pretend that it is possible to distinguish between positive economics (how economies work) and normative economics (how they ought to work). In this vein, they present themselves as dispassionate scientists who will explain to you, like an engineer explains a turbocharger's function, how capitalism works, leaving to philosophers, sociologists, and various cranks the task of discussing how the economy should work. Their implication is that scientific economists should not be influenced by their politics or philosophy, in the same way that you could have a Nazi physicist, as in the 1930s and '40s, and a communist physicist or a liberal physicist who hate each other's political philosophies but, when it comes to the laws of nature, agree because atoms and quanta function in ways that are strictly independent of our ideas about society and humanity. Thus, academic economists gained a lot of discursive power by pretending that they could distinguish and separate the science of economics (the description of how capitalism works) from our ideas of how society ought to be structured.

The problem is, as you know, that the application of natural science methods in social science produces bad natural science and terrible economics. Let's see why. If you're going to be a scientist of society, you might try to emulate the methods of physics. What were the methods of physics that succeeded in imparting so much discursive power to, say, Isaac Newton? The method begins with axioms, statements that one takes for granted before knowing whether they are right or wrong. Take, for example, the principle of energy conservation, Newton's intuition that energy does not dissipate into nothing, that it is not born out of nothing, but rather, it is constant and simply changes form from kinetic to thermal and so on. Newtown had no evidence initially that this was so—it was an axiom. Then he worked out the mathematical relationship between velocity, acceleration, mass, etc., that is consisent with his axiom. This mathematical relationship could then be checked empirically in some laboratory. If it was found to be not inconsistent with the empirical data, Newton could claim, "I have proof that nature works in a manner that is consistent with my axiom—at least so far!" That's the beauty of physics and the reason it excited progressive people who wanted freedom from superstition and an objective method for ascertaining truth.

The economists who became the first professors of economics, the first recognized "scientists of society," emulated that process. That meant they needed to come up with their own axioms. If you're going to have a universal axiom about how humans function (equivalent to Newton's energy conservation principle), one that applies equally in Britain, in Palestine, in the distant parts of the galaxy, you need to come up with a very general proposition. For instance, "Humans do whatever maximizes their utility function." But this is a tautology, like saying that I do what I like and I like what I do. Still, it allowed academic economists to write down mathematical equations describing human behavior, consumer choice, and producer choice. Thus they produced their own systems of equations.

216 | PALESTINE IN A WORLD ON FIRE

But that's where the comparison with physics ends, for two reasons: First, we do not have proper laboratories to test macroeconomic propositions (eg, had the central bank not printed money, there would have been no inflation). Second, even the labs we do have can never test the theory of human behavior when some economists, when confronted by data showing Jill and Jack violate the economists' theory of how Jill and Jack ought to behave, turn around and blame the negative result on Jill's and Jack's irrationality rather than accept that their theory was bunk.

When I was studying all this back in the 1970s and 1980s, what fascinated me was that the very same unrealistic axioms that are necessary to "close" their models (in order to get tenure and embark on brilliant academic careers) were the very same assumptions that financiers used to "close" their financial models. The same models would reappear later behind the construction of the derivatives by Lehman Brothers and Goldman Sachs that blew up in 2008. The more antiscientific you were in order to solve your mathematical models, and the more you distanced yourself from actually existing capitalism, the more successful you became as an economist. Which, of course, made sense, given that the more functional your models were to the fictional capital generated by finananciers, the more money you brought to your economics department (as grants from the financiers), and the greater your likelihood of success in the profession, even being awarded a Nobel Prize in economics.

That is what I call a most peculiar failure. It is *as if* there is a whole system of incentives to produce bad economics. *As if* there exists a system designed to procure misleading models. Of course, no one designed such a system; it evolved spontaneously. The economics profession is best thought of as a priesthood that reproduces itself through particular practices that its members perform earnestly, in a manner that, supraintentionally (a little like Adam Smith's invisible hand), leads to the permanent and irreversible disengagement between economic theory and really existing capitalism.

If I am right that this disconnect between economic reality and economic theory is baked into economics, is it any wonder that when Western finance crashed and burned in 2008, Queen Elizabeth [II] asked the members of the Royal Economic Society, "Why didn't you see it coming?" and they had no idea? It took them days to come up with a groveling letter of apology saying, "Our models couldn't tell us." Of course they couldn't tell you because they were designed *not* to tell you. Your models were designed not to have anything useful or relevant to say about actually existing capitalism, and this is why you were so powerful in the academe and beyond. There is, in other words, a fundamental and profound difference between saying that economics failed and my hypothesis that economics is designed to acquire discursive power in our academy and in society at large in proportion to its incapacity to understand capitalism.

How can we escape this trap? What should we be providing our students instead of a diet of mathematically interesting models that obfuscate the economy we live in? The solution is certainly not to ignore these models, since they are the language spoken in the corridors of power (treasury, central banks, boardrooms, etc.). No, the answer is to teach these models in the same way we teach the history of religion. The same way you explain, for instance, what happened to precipitate the schism between the Catholic Church and the Orthodox Church, and therefore to bring on the Crusades that ravaged Palestine. Yes, by all means, speak to students about the clashes on and around the doctrine of Filioque (whether the Holy Spirit is moved about by the will of God or of God and Christ simultaneously), but do so in the context of the deep, underlying commercial wars between the Western and Eastern remnants of the Roman Empire (centered upon Rome and Constantinople respectively) underpinning the theological clashes on who moves, who doesn't, the Holy Spirit.

ILAN PAPPÉ: Maybe this is a moment to move to a related issue: the situation that emerged in both the economic and political world under the COVID-19 pandemic.

In a dystopian mood, some of us fear that what you call rightly "technofeudalism" is collaborating with, or may be replaced or augmented by, biofeudalism. Pharmaceutical giants are developing research with taxpayers' money, producing and selling solutions in the name of public health and under the panic of a pandemic. Corporations' share prices rise in the stock exchange markets while the number of unemployed, working, and middle-class people is unprecedented all over the world. The same is true about companies that produce surveillance products.

Do you have an antidote that might help us to see the pandemic reality as a moment of hope rather than despair? An optimism that would potentially justify the question mark on the title of your book *And the Weak Suffer What They Must?* Do you see a ray of hope coming from the pandemic in terms of the global economy, in the near and more distant future?

YANIS VAROUFAKIS: I always see hope wherever I look. Whether it was the 2008 crisis or the pandemic or even ghastly wars, hope is everywhere. When you look into the eyes of the young who are resisting climate change or trade unionists rising up in New Jersey and Bangladesh against working conditions in Amazon's warehouses or into the the eyes of traumatized children in Palestine, hope is always there.

Speaking of biofeudalism, it too is part of technofeudalism. I'm not simply talking about digital technologies but the capacity of high tech, whether it's bio high tech or digital high tech, to aid and abet the creation of a new kind of feudalism. Is there an antidote to globalized technofeudalism? Of course. And it takes the form of internationalist, democratic movements.

Some of us have come together in what we call the Progressive International—it all started in November 2018 in Vermont, when Bernie Sanders and I called for people to join in a Progressive International. Now it has been taken over by movements from around the world: from Africa, Asia, Latin America, the United States, and here in Europe. For me, the Progressive International is a great source of hope because, let's face it: The bankers and the fascists have internationalized. Modi, Salvini, Le Pen, Trump, Bolsonaro, and Netanyahu fully understand the power of solidarity. Similarly, if you go to Davos you will find bankers and oligarchs sitting around the table from different countries: from England, Switzerland, Thailand, Nigeria. There is no hint of racism or discrimination among them. They're like brothers and sisters. Isn't it time that we internationalists do the same?

Now, since you asked about technofeudalism, let me offer a brief explanation of the term, as I understand and mean it. At the beginning of the twentieth century, the rosy view of capitalism as a competitive, village-like marketplace in which the baker, the brewer, and the butcher (three iconic figures who feature in Adam Smith's account of free markets) had already been sidelined by large corporations like the networked firms of Thomas Edison and Henry Ford. We had already moved to what Rosa Luxemburg, Lenin, and others referred to as "monopoly capitalism." But in 2008 there was a structural shift away from that. Some friends, colleagues, and comrades of mine are somehow puzzled by my insistence that 2008 was for capitalism what 1991 was to the Soviet Union and its satellites. But after 2008, I submit to you, we are no longer in a standard monopoly capitalist environment.

Ford, General Electric, and Walmart are good examples of monopolies that, after the Second World War, regrouped (under the Bretton Woods system) to become what John Kenneth Galbraith referred to as the Technostructure. The Technostructure was a form of central planning involving a cartel of industrialists—the highest form of monopoly capitalism, if you will. A new managerial class had emerged within the US war economy, and they ran, at once, the US entrepreneurial state and the private conglomerates. Weaponizing smart marketing and clever advertising, they generated the products, the innovations, and the desires of consumers for these commodities. However, the Technostructure's foundation was still capitalist in the sense that the basic force driving the world economy was surplus value realized from the labor process—from the disparity between the value of labor going into commodities and services by workers, and the value of their labor time wages.

The standard process of capital accumulation—of capitalist production yielding surplus value, part of which ended up as profits for capitalists, which then drove the system—was maintained even during the phase of monopoly capitalism that people like Paul Sweezy and my friends from *Monthly Review* in New York were beautifully mapping out. However, it is my contention that in 2008 the underlying dynamic of the Technostructure's capital accumulation buckled under under the weight of the financial sector's hubris. Central banks came in and started pumping rivers of cash into finance. Their aim was temporarily to refloat the financial sector, but in practicing what I call "socialism for the financiers" and huge austerity for everyone else across the Western world, they squeezed aggregate demand, curtailed investment in physical capital, and thus zombified corporations and banks while devastating both the West's proletariat and middle classes. So, effectively, we ended up with a financial sphere that was doing very well, financially, but also with conglomerates whose financial health was not related to their profitability.

The pandemic was not responsible for capitalism's stagnation, but it turbocharged it nevertheless. Indeed, the pandemic accelerated and deepened a process that had begun already under Obama and his administration's audacious refloating of the financial sector in 2009. From 2009 till the pandemic's end, the process was straightforward to understand: Central banks were printing oodles of cash to hand over to the private banks. The private banks were never going to lend the cash to austerity-hit "little people" (eg, small businesses, working- and middle-class families) because universal austerity meant that the "little" people could not be relied upon to repay it. So the bankers picked up the phone and called their mates at large conglomerates like Apple in the US, Volkswagen in Germany, Alstom in France, and said, "Look, I have a load of cash that the central bank has given me at negative interest rates—so I can give it to you for free, at a zero interest rate, and still make a profit. Do you want it?"

These corporations did not plan to invest any money. They could also see that the "little" people could not afford high value–added products. So they would not invest money even if it fell upon them like manna from heaven. Recall the large piles of savings that these conglomerates were sitting on—for the first time in the history of capitalism, corporations had savings! Corporations are not meant to have savings. Households are supposed to save, while corporations borrow to invest. So when you see that Apple had $200 billion as savings, and similar with European corporations, you should immediately think: "My god, something's going wrong here."

Naturally, the corporations offered free money from their bankers did not turn down the free central bank money. They took it and headed straight for the stock exchange to buy their own shares. They all did it. Apple took the central bank money, via the private banks, and purchased Apple shares. Volkswagen purchased Volkswagen shares. The share markets skyrocketed, obviously. There was, in the language of Wall Street, an "everything rally." Even when the pandemic shut everyone down and profits disappeared, the financial markets were going gangbusters. You can see why: on the strength of the central bank monies!

If you have any doubt, consider what happened in London on August 12, 2020. At 9:05 a.m., the unprecedented news came out that the markets had not predicted: the UK's national income (GDP) had fallen by more than 20 percent for the first time in the history of British capitalism. That was way above the national income drop the markets had expected. Fifteen minutes later, the London Stock Exchange went up! What had happened? Simple: the financiers thought, "Oh, the news is so bad that it must be excellent!"

How could it be good news when national income fell to unexpected lows? The London Stock Exchange went up because financiers were surprised by how . . . bad things were. This phenomenon only makes sense if we come to terms with the fact that we no longer live in what we used to understand as capitalism, if we accept that we live in a world where the financiers thought along the following lines: "Things are *really* awful. But this is great news for us because it means that the Bank of England will panic and start printing even more money to give *us*. Time to rejoice! Since people like us—fincaniers—will suspect that people like us will take all this fresh central bank money to the stock market to buy whatever we can get out hands on, share prices will rise. Time to buy!"

This decoupling of financial wealth creation from capitalism and capitalist profits is one (and not even the most poignant) inkling that this is no longer capitalism. Then there is the new form of capital (which, in my recent book *Technofeudalism: What Killed*

Capitalism I refer to as "cloud capital"), which, using algorithms running on networked machines, modifies our behavior and offers its owners a spectacular capacity to bypass markets and to siphon off surplus value as a new form of rent ("cloud rent," I call it). Add to that biotechnologies that combine so powerfully with the decline of public health services to deliver whole populations to the rent-seeking behavior of biofeudal firms. Firms like Pfizer and Moderna now have immense power over society because they are producing the stuff that saves lives in societies where the national health service is delivered to them giftwrapped.

To give you one last reason why I am, controversially, arguing that this is no longer capitalism but a variety of technofeudalism, think of the moment you enter Amazon. I wish to argue that at that moment, the moment you are in Amazon, you have exited capitalism. It is as if you've stepped out onto the commercial road of your town, the High Street, as the English would say, or Main Street in America, you looked around and you found yourself in a dystopian science fiction movie: You realize that every building, every shop, every house is owned by one person. That whatever is sold there is controlled by that one person, who has played no role in its production. The (digital) air you breathe in that digital platform, the digital tarmac on which you walk, the digital bench on which you sit to rest—they all belong to that one person. A person who, courtesy of owning this digital universe and the algorithm that controls everything within it, is far more than a mere monopolist—he determines which products you see and which you can't, whom you can talk to and who is out of your reach, what you can buy and at what price you can buy it. It is the same person who charges the producer of whatever you buy up to 40 percent of the final price. And, as if that were not enough, this is the person who lures you into investing your free labor into updating his digital (or cloud) capital with your reviews, likes, posts, videos, and data. This is not capitalism, I submit to you and to our readers, dear Ilan. Welcome to technofeudalism!

I hope that you can now see why I claim that, since 2008, we have been living in world that is rapidly becoming technofeudal. Moreover, this technofeudal world is exceptionally fragile and more unstable than even capitalism was. In this world, the greatest threat to the many, to the *demos*, is that we shall mistake this totalitarian system as a liberal, powerful, solid, natural system—which it is not. The power of the Jeff Bezoses of the world, of the Zuckerbergs, of the owners of Pfizer is the false belief in the minds of the many that we are the powerless ones. Our duty, therefore, is to let people across the world in on a crucial, liberating secret: That everything could be otherwise, as David Graeber used to say. That we, the "little" people, have the power.

AFTERWORD

Ilan Pappé

As this book reached its final stages, the Hamas operation "Al-Aqsa Flood" broke out. What began with a military success of breaching Gaza's ghetto wall, occupying military bases, and capturing soldiers deteriorated into a set of atrocities and war crimes committed by Hamas fighters who entered nearby Jewish settlements and targeted a music festival. It is estimated that among the 1,200 killed on October 7, 2023, around three hundred were Israeli soldiers.[1]

The picture is still not fully known, but the revengeful Israeli reaction has been clear: months of endless bombardment of Gaza, which many observers rightly describe as genocide.[2] At the time of revising our book in May 2024, the number of Palestinians killed exceeds thirty thousand, with over eighty thousand injured, more than 1.7 million internally displaced, and famine immanent.[3]

These terrible events have acted as a magnifying glass, focusing attention on many of the issues discussed with guests in our conversation series. From the alliances and flows of capital that underpin geopolitics, to how settler colonization targets and permeates the senses, themes from our dialogues have enabled us to name and confront power. And to call our community to action. With Palestine on fire once more, it seemed that the world was willing to look at violence as much more than a local outburst, for however long we could succeed in insisting that they do not turn away.

World reactions to the events of October 7 and its aftermath have been largely divided into two modes or camps. The first response is offered by "global Israel" and the second belongs to "global Palestine." By "global Israel," I refer to a coalition that includes most governments in the Global North, some governments of the Global South, dominant media, and mainstream academia, aided by multinational corporations, security companies, military industries, and other capitalist interests. Politically, the most vocal members of this alliance are the right and neo-right factions, but it also enjoys the support of most European social democratic parties and many members of the US Democratic Party.

"Global Israel" has not deviated from the Israeli narrative of the October events. According to this narrative, the attack is yet another chapter in the history of modern antisemitism, this time carried out with a brutality compared to that of the Nazis and organizations like the Islamic State. And, of course, it was allegedly planned in Tehran by the Iranian regime. As horrific as it is, comparing the killing of 1,200 people to the industrial genocide of six million is the worst abuse of Holocaust memory I can think of, and one that would please Holocaust deniers around the world. The fact the Iran was alarmed by the Hamas operation, as it threatened to ignite an unwanted regional war, did not appear to confuse those who concocted this narrative.

"Global Palestine" reacted differently. This coalition of civil societies from around the globe works in tandem with oppressed minorities, governments of the Global South, and human rights organizations—all express unconditional solidarity with the Palestinian struggle for liberation. As a movement, "global Palestine" has gained increasing support and reached unprecedented popularity in recent years, including among its ranks people from all walks of life. With varying degrees of commitment, members support the Boycott, Divestment, Sanctions (BDS) movement, a one-state future, and Palestinian refugees' right of return.

The position of "global Palestine" was noted by the liberal left in Israel. On a daily basis, *Haaretz,* Israel's most prominent and broadly left-leaning newspaper, attacked what it called the immoral position of the "global left" and named some of our own interlocuters. Their sin, according to the liberal Zionists, was twofold. First, in providing historical context for the events, they defined Zionism as settler colonialism. Second, they offered a moral context that pointed to violence committed by past anticolonial and anti-oppression movements, without invalidating or questioning the justice of these struggles.

It is useful to identify "global Israel" and "global Palestine" in this moment, even as we must also attend to the spaces between and beyond them. For as horrific as the past several months have been in the history of Palestine and Israel, they are not likely to change the material and political reality. Palestinian refugees will continue to be denied their internationally recognized right of return; Palestinian citizens of Israel will continue to live in an apartheid Jewish state; the West Bank will continue to be occupied and colonized; and Gaza will continue to be at the mercy of Israel, whatever the outcome of these terrible months. We will continue to need global Palestine as the banner under which we organize in the face of global Israel and its power. The fire will rage on.

And still, we must have hope. I hope that this book will contribute to the just struggle that "global Palestine" supports—a movement for liberation and self-determination that connects Palestine with other struggles across the globe. This is the kind of internationalism and intersectional solidarity called for by those scholars, activists, educators, and organizers who joined us in thinking with, learning from, caring for, and insisting on Palestine. Their knowledge and experience—curiosity, determination, and sometimes failure—teach us to forge tools for fighting the flames that surround us. And to build the world anew.

ACKNOWLEDGMENTS

Palestine in a World on Fire is deeply indebted to the work of a collective, who organized to make possible moments of togetherness in a time of immeasurable loss. At the height of the COVID-19 pandemic, we gathered to listen to and learn from some of the most visionary, radical voices holding academia accountable to political realities, everyday life, and powerful ideals such as "justice" and "internationalism." We met in the evenings (UK-time)—which were mornings, afternoons, and late nights in the locations from which our audiences joined us—and we paused. To center Palestine, to trace connections, to think beyond the limits of what seems possible. And to renew our commitment to work together in pursuit of transformation.

This project, a conversation series, unfolded over two years and owes much to the generosity, creativity, and skill of friends and comrades. We would like to thank those who chaired each conversation with grace and wisdom, hosting our guests and facilitating discussion: Asha Ali, Colter Louwerse, Sajjad Rizvi, Roba al-Salibi, Clara El Akiki, Kanwal Hameed, Adam Hanieh, Neha Shaji, Lara Choksey, Malcolm Richards, Francesco Amoruso, Bryar Bajalan, Tina Phillips, Rami Rmeileh, Natalie Ohana, Hashem Abushama, Nandini Chatterjee, Lara Fricke, and Sabiha Allouche. We also owe much gratitude to the technical team who came together to enable our online meetings to become intimate global conversations—while others are thanked above, Andrea Wallace was key to ensuring a smooth production and a warm atmosphere of exchange. We also wish to acknowledge those who helped at the virtual "door" and made each event a truly inclusive experience: Finlay Carroll, Riadh Ghemmour, and Tinashe Verhaeghe, among others named previously.

Our series also benefited from the expertise in technology and communication brought together by the University of Exeter. In particular we thank Melanie Shaw, Helen Gilhespy, Emma Clark, Toby Squire, and the broader University IT and Events Teams. The important work of spreading the word was undertaken by Nadia Khalaf, Sarah Roberts, Sarah Wood, Safi Darden, and Joseph Sweetman, whose connections and knowledge enabled these conversations to reach—and include—people across the globe. Our gratitude also extends to the assistants supporting our guests: Cassandra Shaylor, Aspasia Feggouli, Stephanie Lee, and Surya Parkeh. And we wish to thank Pascale Walker for the use of her original artwork.

We are also grateful to our organizational and institutional partners, namely the Exeter Decolonizing Network (EDN), the European Centre for Palestine Studies (ECPS), the Institute of Arab and Islamic Studies (IAIS), and the University of Exeter. We are especially appreciative of Professor Gareth Stansfield's work in championing the conversation series and insisting on its significance to university leadership.

Yet the "work" of this project is perhaps most indebted to our students, whose visions of the future inspire us to meet, to ask questions, to seek wisdom, to listen, and to do. This book is for you.

SELECTED BIBLIOGRAPHY

Abdo, Nahla, and Nur Masalha, eds. *An Oral History of the Palestinian Nakba*. London: Zed Books, 2018.

Abu-Lughod, Lila, Rema Hammami, and Nadera Shalhoub-Kevorkian, eds. *The Cunning of Gender Violence: Geopolitics and Feminism*. Durham & London: Duke University Press, 2023.

Ahmed, Sara. *Queer Phenomenology: Orientations, Objects, Others*. Durham & London: Duke University Press, 2006.

Ahmed, Sara. *Living a Feminist Life*. Durham & London: Duke University Press, 2017.

Alcalay, Ammiel. *After Jews and Arabs: Remaking Levantine Culture*. Minneapolis: University of Minnesota Press, 1992.

Allen, Lori. *A History of False Hope: Investigative Commissions in Palestine*. Redwood City, CA: Stanford University Press, 2020.

Al-Qaisiya, Walaa. "Decolonial Queering: The Politics of Being Queer in Palestine." *Journal of Palestine Studies* 47, no. 3 (2018): 29–44.

Arendt, Hannah. *Eichmann in Jerusalem: A Report on the Banality of Evil*. London: Penguin Classics, 2006 (1963).

Arvin, Maile, Eve Tuck, and Angie Morrill. "Decolonizing Feminism: Challenging Connections between Settler Colonialism and Heteropatriarchy." *Feminist Formations* 25, no. 1 (2013): 8–34. DOI: 10.1353/ff.2013.0006.

Barakat, Rana. "Writing/Righting Palestine Studies: Settler Colonialism, Indigenous Sovereignty and Resisting the Ghost(s) of History." *Settler Colonial Studies* 8, no. 3 (2018): 349–63. DOI: 10.1080/2201473X.2017.1300048.

Buber, Martin. *I and Thou*. Translated by Ronald Gregor Smith. New York: Scribner Book Company, 2000 (1923).

Bulley, Dan, Jenny Edkins, and Nadine El-Enany. *After Grenfell: Violence, Resistance and Response*. London: Pluto Press, 2019.

Butler, Judith. *Gender Trouble: Feminism and the Subversion of Identity*.

London: Routledge, 2006 (1990).

Chomsky, Noam, and Ilan Pappé. *On Palestine*. London: Penguin Books, 2015.

Davis, Angela Y., and Cassandra Shaylor. "Race, Gender and the Prison Industrial Complex in California and Beyond." *Meridians* 2, no. 1 (2001): 1–25. https://www.jstor.org/stable/40338793.

El-Enany, Nadine. *(B)ordering Britain: Law, Race and Empire*. Manchester: Manchester University Press, 2018.

Erakat, Noura. *Justice for Some: Law and the Question of Palestine*. Redwood City, CA: Stanford University Press, 2019.

Fanon, Frantz. *Wretched of the Earth*. Translated by Contance Farrington. London: Penguin Classics, 2001 (1961).

Gilroy, Paul. *The Black Atlantic: Modernity and Double Consciousness*. London: Verso Books, 1993.

Gilroy, Paul. "The Myth of Black Criminality." *Socialist Register* 19 (1982): 47–56.

Halberstam, Jack. *The Queer Art of Failure*. Durham & London: Duke University Press, 2011.

Jiryis, Sabri, and Salah Qallab. "The Palestine Research Center." *Journal of Palestine Studies* 14, no. 4 (1985): 185–87. DOI: https://doi. org/10.2307/2537147.

Jordan, June. *Driven by Desire: The Collected Poems of June Jordan*. Port Townsend, WA: Copper Canyon Press, 2007.

Khoury, Elias. *Broken Mirrors: Sinalcol*. London: MacLehose Press, 2015.

Khoury, Elias. *Children of the Ghetto: My Name Is Adam*. New York: Archipelago Books, 2019.

Khoury, Elias. *Gate of the Sun*. Translated by Humphrey Davies. London: Vintage, 2006.

Klein, Naomi. *The Shock Doctrine: The Rise of Disaster Capitalism*. London: Penguin Books, 2008.

Makdisi, Ussama. *Age of Coexistence: The Ecumenical Frame and the Making of the Modern Arab World*. Oakland: University of California Press, 2021.

Massad, Joseph. "Re-Orienting Desire: The Gay International and the Arab World." *Public Culture* 14, no. 2 (2002): 361–85.

Million, Dian. "Felt Theory: An Indigenous Feminist Approach to Affect and History." *Wicazo Sa Review* 24, no. 2 (2009): 53–76. DOI: 10.1353/wic.0.0043.

Natanel, Katherine. "Affect, Excess and Settler Colonialism in Palestine/Israel." *Settler Colonial Studies* 13, no. 3 (2023): 325–48. DOI: 10.1080/2201473X.2022.2112427.

Pappé, Ilan. "Everyday Evil in Palestine: The View from Lucifer's Hill." *Janus Unbound, Journal of Critical Studies* 1, no. 1 (2021): 70–82.

Rao, Rahul. "Queer Questions." *International Feminist Journal of Politics* 16, no. 2 (2014): 199–217. DOI: 10.1080/14616742.2014.901817.

Razack, Sherene. "Stealing Pain of Others: Reflections on Canadian Humanitarian Responses." *Review of Education, Pedagogy and Cultural Studies* 29, no. 4 (2007): 375–94. DOI: 10.1080/10714410701454198.

Ritchie, Jason. "Black Skin Splits: The Birth (and Death) of the Queer Palestinian." In *Queer Necropolitics*, edited by Jin Haritaworn, Adi Kuntsman, and Silvia Posocco, 111–28. London: Routledge, 2014.

Robinson, Cedric. *Black Marxism: The Making of the Black Radical Tradition.* London: Penguin Classics, 2021 (1983).

Rouhana, Nadim, and Nadera Shalhoub-Kevorkian, eds. *When Politics Are Sacralized: Comparative Perspectives on Religious Claims and Nationalism.* Cambridge: Cambridge University Press, 2021.

Said, Edward. *Orientalism.* London: Penguin Books, 2003 (1978).

Said, Edward. "Permission to Narrate." *Journal of Palestine Studies* 13, no. 3, (1984): 27–48. DOI: 10.2307/2536688.

Shalhoub-Kevorkian, Nadera. "The Occupation of the Senses: The Prosthetic and Aesthetic of State Terror." *British Journal of Criminology* 57, no. 6 (2017): 1279–1300. https://doi.org/10.1093/bjc/azw066.

Shalhoub-Kevorkian, Nadera. *Security Theology, Surveillance and the Politics of Fear.* Cambridge: Cambridge University Press, 2015.

Shaw, Flora. *A Tropical Dependency: An Outline of the Ancient History of the Western Sudan with an Account of the Modern Settlement of Northern Nigeria.* Baltimore, MD: Black Classic Press, 1995 (1905).

Sheehi, Lara, and Stephen Sheehi. *Psychoanalysis under Occupation: Practicing Resistance in Palestine.* London: Routledge, 2021.

Simpson, Audra. "On Ethnographic Refusal: Indigeneity, 'Voice' and Colonial Citizenship." *Junctures: The Journal for Thematic Dialogue,* no. 9 (2007): 67–80.

Spivak, Gayatri Chakravorty. *An Aesthetic Education in the Era of Globalization.* Cambridge, MA: Harvard University Press, 2013.

Spivak, Gayatri Chakravorty. "Can the Subaltern Speak?" In *Marxism and the Interpretation of Culture,* edited by Cary Nelson and Lawrence Grossberg, 271–313. Basingstoke, UK: Macmillan, 1988.

Varoufakis, Yanis. *And the Weak Suffer What They Must? Europe's Crisis and America's Economic Future.* New York: Nation Books, 2016.

Yizhar, S. *Khirbet Khizeh.* Translated by Nicholas de Lange and Yaacob Dweck. London: Granta Books, 2011 (1949).

NOTES

INTRODUCTION

1. Many thanks to Bill Mullen for seeing the worth of these conversations so sharply in his preliminary review of our manuscript.

2. For a summary of the George Floyd case, see "How George Floyd Died, and What Happened Next," *New York Times*, July 29, 2022, https://www.nytimes.com/article/george-floyd.html. On the removal of Colston's statute, see Tristan Cork, "How the City Failed to Remove Edward Colston's Statue for Years," *Bristol Post*, January 5, 2022, https://www.bristolpost.co.uk/news/bristol-news/how-city-failed-remove-edward-4211771.

3. As readers will note, our book adopts an alphabetical order—rather than chronological—to create a more democratic, fluid, and collective structure. Our gratitude again goes to Bill Mullen for his encouragement.

4. All transcripts have been edited for length and clarity.

5. This section also owes much to Sara Ahmed's *Living a Feminist Life*, which concludes with "A Killjoy Survival Kit," (Durham, NC: Duke University Press, 2017), 235–50. So, too, it takes inspiration from Maile Arvin, Eve Tuck, and Angie Morrill's "Decolonizing Feminism: Challenging Connections between Settler Colonialism and Heteropatriarchy," *Feminist Formations* 25, no. 1 (Spring 2013): 8–34.

6. Edward Said, "Permission to Narrate," *Journal of Palestine Studies* 13, no. 3 (1984): 27–48, https://doi.org/10.2307/2536688; Rana Barakat, " Writing/Righting Palestine Studies: Settler Colonialism, Indigenous Sovereignty and Resisting the Ghost(s) of History," *Settler Colonial Studies* 8, no. 3 (2018): 349–63, DOI: 10.1080/2201473X.2017.1300048.

7. From Sara Ahmed, *Queer Phenomenology: Orientations, Objects, Others* (Durham: Duke University Press, 2006), 44.

8. An explanation of the term can be found in Ilan Pappé, "Everyday Evil in Palestine: The View from Lucifer's Hill," *Janus Unbound, Journal of Critical Studies* 1, no. 1 (Fall 2021): 70–82.

9. See, for example, the work collected in Nahla Abdo and Nur Masalha, eds.,

An Oral History of the Palestinian Nakba (London: Zed Books, 2018).

10. See Sabri Jiryis and Salah Qallab, "The Palestine Research Center," *Journal of Palestine Studies* 14, no. 4 (Summer 1985): 185–87.

11. This portion of Davis's comments took place during the question and answer period of the conversation, which has been omitted from the transcript in this book.

12. The work of Indigenous scholars like Dian Million (2009), Sherene Razack (2007), and Audra Simpson (2007) alerts us to the history of silencing and erasure while insisting on the value of feeling to our political realities and futures.

13. See, for example, Katherine Natanel's "Affect, Excess and Settler Colonialism in Palestine/Israel," *Settler Colonial Studies* 13, no. 3 (2023): 325–48.

14. Jack Halberstam, *The Queer Art of Failure* (Durham & London: Duke University Press, 2011), 2–3.

15. See *Driven by Desire: The Collected Poems of June Jordan* (Port Townsend, WA: Copper Canyon Press 2007).

16. "What We Do," Counter Terrorism Policing, https://www.counterterrorism.police.uk/what-we-do/prevent/.

17. "Working Definition of Holocaust Denial and Distortion," International Holocaust Remembrance Alliance, https://www.holocaustremembrance.com/resources/working-definitions-charters/working-definition-holocaust-denial-and-distortion.

18. This quotation also comes from the question and answer portion of our conversation with Angela Davis.

MUSTAFA BARGHOUTI: LIBERATION AND THE LEFT

1. For more on the 2021 uprising, see Akram Salhab and Dahoud al-Ghoul, "Jerusalem Youth at the Forefront of 2021's Unity Intifada," *Middle East Report Online*, November 10, 2021, https://merip.org/2021/11/jerusalem-youth-at-the-forefront-of-2021s-unity-intifada/.

2. See Yumna Patel, "What's Happening in the Naqab? Israel Uproots Palestinians to Plant Trees," Mondoweiss, January 14, 2022, https://mondoweiss.net/2022/01/whats-happening-in-the-naqab-israel-uproots-palestinians-to-plant-trees/.

ANGELA Y. DAVIS: TOWARD TRANSNATIONAL MOVEMENTS FOR JUSTICE

1. "What Is the PIC? What Is Abolition?" Critical Resistance, https://criticalresistance.org/mission-vision/not-so-common-language/.

2. See Angela Y. Davis and Cassandra Shaylor, "Race, Gender and the Prison Industrial Complex in California and Beyond," *Meridians* 2, no. 1 (2001): 1–25.

3. In *The Shock Doctrine* (2008), Klein proposes "disaster capitalism" as

the social and economic strategy that uses crises, whether driven by humans or nature, to advance radical privatization.

4. For recent statistics on private prisons in the United States, see work by the Sentencing Project: https://www.sentencingproject.org/. This includes Kristen M. Budd and Niki Monazzam, "Private Prisons in the United States," Sentencing Project, June 15, 2023, https://www. sentencingproject.org/reports/private-prisons-in-the-united-states/.

NADINE EL-ENANY: ON COLONIAL VIOLENCE AND ANTICOLONIAL RESISTANCE

1. Between May 10 and May 21, 2021, the Israeli military attacked Gaza with airstrikes and shelling, killing over 250 people and injuring more than two thousand. See "Gaza: Apparent War Crimes during May Fighting," Human Rights Watch, July 27, 2021, https://www.hrw.org/news/2021/07/27/gaza-apparent-war-crimes-during-may-fighting. Violence also escalated in Jerusalem and across the West Bank during this time, including house evictions, settler attacks, repression of protest, and restriction of access to holy sites.

2. In 2018, the Windrush scandal brought to public attention how legislation and law enforcement targeted a generation of Commonwealth citizens in the UK, depriving them of health care and threatening hundreds with deportation. These practices aligned with the "hostile environment" policies that aimed to deter immigration. See Amelia Gentleman, "Windrush Scandal Caused by '30 Years of Racist Immigration Laws' – Report," *Guardian*, May 29, 2022, https://www.theguardian.com/uk-news/2022/may/29/windrush-scandal-caused-by-30-years-of-racist-immigration-laws-report.

3. These decades saw a concerted attempt by the UK state and its police force to violently quash the Black Power movement. This included the arrest and trial of Black youths and activists in the 1970s, such as the Mangrove Nine, and the Bristol and Brixton riots of the 1980s. See Paul Gilroy, "The Myth of Black Criminality," *Social Register* 19 (1982): 47–56.

4. Following the toppling of Edward Colston's statue in Bristol, campaigners in Oxford called for the removal of British imperialist Cecil Rhodes's statue at Oriel College. While Oriel's governing body indicated that the statue would be removed in 2020, they later claimed that "regulatory and financial challenges" prevented this from happening. See Michael Race, "Cecil Rhodes Statue Will Not Be Removed by Oxford College," BBC, May 20, 2021, https://www.bbc.co.uk/news/uk-england-oxfordshire-57175057.

5. Passed in 2022, this bill introduced new powers for the police, restricted protest, and criminalized transient ways of life. The Kill the Bill movement galvanized widespread protests across the UK in response. See Megan Specia, "What Are the 'Kill the Bill' Protests in Britain All About?" *New York Times*, March 23, 2021, https://www.nytimes.com/2021/03/23/

world/europe/kill-the-bill-protests-uk.html.

6. Commission on Race and Ethnic Disparities, "Commission on Race and Ethnic Disparities: The Report," 2021, https://assets.publishing.service. gov.uk/media/6062ddb1d3bf7f5ce1060aa4/20210331_-_CRED_Report_-_FINAL_-_Web_Accessible.pdf.

7. For 2023 guidance, see Home Office, "Prevent Duty Guidance: England and Wales (2023)," https://www.gov.uk/government/publications/prevent-duty-guidance.

8. Home Office, "Counter-Terrorism and Security Act," 2015, https://www. gov.uk/government/collections/counter-terrorism-and-security-bill. The Prevent duty falls under Section 29 of this act.

9. Hélène Cixous in Hélène Cixous and Catherine Clément, *The Newly Born Woman* (Minneapolis: University of Minnesota Press [1975] 1986), 72.

10. Paul Beaumont, "ICC Opens Investigation into War Crimes in Palestinian Territories," *Guardian*, March 3, 2021, https://www.theguardian.com/law/2021/mar/03/icc-open-formal-investigation-war-crimes-palestine.

PAUL GILROY: HISTORIES FOR THE FUTURE

1. This agreement was signed between Britain and France on April 11, 1713, as part of the treaties (the Peace of Utrecht) that ended the War of the Spanish Succession. Its significance here rests partly in the principle of the balance of power, which prevented the union of monarchies as crucial to the preservation of peace. In later practice, the treaty became a basis for framing concrete legal rights and obligations.

2. Adopted by the Ninth International Conference of American States on May 2, 1948, in Bogota, Colombia, the declaration outlines individual human rights in social, economic, and cultural spheres, as well as equality under the law. It advocates for the protection and promotion of fundamental rights, though it is not legally binding.

3. This declaration was proclaimed by the United Nations General Assembly on December 10, 1948, setting out fundamental human rights to be universally protected.

4. Published in 1689, Locke's *Second Treatise* provides the basis for liberalism as a political philosophy.

5. See *Driven by Desire: The Collected Poems of June Jordan* (Port Townsend, WA: Copper Canyon Press, 2007).

ELIAS KHOURY: TIMES OF STRUGGLE AND CULTURAL LIBERATION

1. See "Remembering Basil al-Araj and Continuing His Legacy of Struggle," Palestinian Prisoner Solidarity Network, March 6, 2021, https://samidoun.net/2021/03/remembering-basil-al-araj-and-continuing-his-legacy-of-struggle.

GABOR MATÉ: ON TRAUMA AND (THE LIMITS OF) COMPASSION

1. *Tantura*, directed by Alon Schwartz (2022).

NADERA SHALHOUB-KEVORKIAN: ON LIFE AND DEATH IN PALESTINE

1. Said in Arabic during the conversation.
2. Said in Arabic during the conversation.
3. Said in Arabic during the conversation.

GAYATRI CHAKRAVORTY SPIVAK: COLONIALITY, SUBALTERNITY, AND REVOLUTION IN OUR TIME

1. Focusing on prehistories of globalization, this multi-institution project involves China, India, the United States, five European countries, and the Senegambia region of Africa.
2. From Gayatri Chakravorty Spivak, "Terror: A Speech after 9-11," *boundary 2* 31, no. 2 (Summer 2004): 81–111.

YANIS VAROUFAKIS: ON CRISIS AND DISOBEDIENCE

1. This dialogue was edited for presentation in this volume. "A Conversation with Yanis Faroufakis and Ilan Pappé," May 12, 2021, Institute of Arab and Islamic Studies, https://www.youtube.com/watch?v=D6kAmxkww-s.
2. In May 2021, Israeli prime minister Benjamin Netanyahu authorized and defended police action to violently suppress Palestinian protests and limit access to Al-Aqsa Mosque during Ramadan. These events took place in the midst of Netanyahu's ongoing trial for corruption and a challenge to his power by the "change bloc." See "Jerusalem Protests: Netanyahu Defends Israeli Action after Clashes with Palestinians," BBC, May 9, 2021, https://www.bbc.co.uk/news/world-middle-east-57049126, and Akiva Eldar, "How the Violence Plays into Netanyahu's Hands," Al Jazeera, May 16, 2021, https://www.aljazeera.com/opinions/2021/5/16/how-the-violence-plays-into-netanyahus-hands.

AFTERWORD

1. Aaron Boxerman, "What We Know about the Death Toll in Israel from the Hamas-Led Attacks," *New York Times*, November 12, 2023, https://www.nytimes.com/2023/11/12/world/middleeast/israel-death-toll-hamas-attack.html.
2. "Gaza: UN Experts Call on International Community to Prevent Genocide against the Palestinians," United Nations Human Rights Office of the High Commissioner, press release, November 16, 2023, https://www.ohchr.org/en/press-releases/2023/11/gaza-un-experts-call-international-community-prevent-genocide-against.
3. United Nations Population Fund, "UNFPA Palestine Situation Report #8 – 22 May 2024," https://www.unfpa.org/resources/unfpa-palestine-situation-report-8-22-may-2024.

INDEX

ABOUT THE EDITORS

KATHERINE NATANEL is a senior lecturer in gender studies at the Institute of Arab and Islamic Studies, University of Exeter. Her research engages with political participation and mobilization; conflict and political violence; and affect and political emotions, primarily in the context of Palestine/Israel. Her first book, *Sustaining Conflict: Apathy and Domination in Israel-Palestine*, was awarded the 2017 Feminist and Women's Studies Association (UK & Ireland) Book Prize. Katie is the executive editor for Middle East Research and Information Project (MERIP).

ILAN PAPPÉ is the director of the European Center for Palestine Studies at the University of Exeter and a senior fellow at the Institute of Arab and Islamic Studies in the University of Exeter. Pappé has written twenty-two books to date, including *Our Visions for Liberation*, *The War on Gaza*, *On Palestine*, and the best seller *The Ethnic Cleansing of Palestine*.